The Founders of Modern Finance: Their Prize-winning Concepts and 1990 Nobel Lectures

The Research Foundation of
The Institute of Chartered Financial Analysts

Research Foundation Publications

Canadian Stocks, Bonds, Bills, and Inflation: 1950–1987
by James E. Hatch and Robert E. White

Closed-Form Duration Measures and Strategy Applications
by Nelson J. Lacey and Sanjay K. Nawalkha

Default Risk, Mortality Rates, and the Performance of Corporate Bonds
by Edward I. Altman

Durations of Nondefault-Free Securities
by Gerald O. Bierwag and George G. Kaufman

The Effect of Illiquidity on Bond Price Data: Some Symptoms and Remedies
by Oded Sarig and Arthur Warga

Initial Public Offerings: The Role of Venture Capitalists
by Joseph T. Lim and Anthony Saunders

A New Perspective on Asset Allocation
by Martin L. Leibowitz

The Poison Pill Anti-takeover Defense: The Price of Strategic Deterrence
by Robert F. Bruner

Program Trading and Systematic Risk
by A.J. Senchack, Jr., and John D. Martin

The Role of Risk Tolerance in the Asset Allocation Process: A New Perspective
by W.V. Harlow and Keith C. Brown

Selecting Superior Securities
by Mark R. Reinganum

Stock Market Structure, Volatility, and Volume
by Hans R. Stoll and Robert E. Whaley

Stocks, Bonds, Bills, and Inflation: Historical Returns (1926–1987)
by Roger G. Ibbotson and Rex A. Sinquefield
(Published with Business One Irwin)

The Founders of Modern Finance: Their Prize-winning Concepts and 1990 Nobel Lectures

ISBN 0-943205-10-7

Printed in the United States of America

Joni L. Tomal, *Production Editor*
Jaynee M. Dudley, *Editorial Assistant*
Brett M. Ferguson, *Editorial Assistant*

July 1991

Mission Statement

The mission of the Research Foundation is to identify, fund, and publish research material that:
- expands the body of relevant and useful knowledge available to practitioners;
- assists practitioners in understanding and applying this knowledge; and
- enhances the investment management community's effectiveness in serving clients.

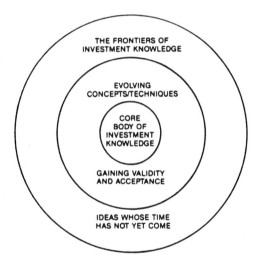

The Research Foundation of
The Institute of Chartered Financial Analysts
P. O. Box 3668
Charlottesville, Virginia 22903
(804) 977-6600

Table of Contents

Foreword

Harry M. Markowitz, Merton H. Miller, and William F. Sharpe earned the 1990 Nobel Prize in Economic Sciences. [1] Because of the significance of that award for all investment practitioners, it is appropriate for the Association for Investment Management and Research (AIMR) and The Research Foundation of the Institute of Chartered Financial Analysts to mark this event by publishing the winners' seminal works and their 1990 acceptance speeches. Our intellectual debt to them is great. They are, after all is said and done, the founders of modern financial economics and the originators of much of our present-day investment constructs.

This occasion also affords an opportunity to speculate on what "our" Nobel Laureates have wrought. No attempt is made here to balance the accounts individually; instead, their contributions are treated ensemble and melded with those who built on their pioneering efforts. [2] If more enthusiasm, emotion, and exaggeration are present than protocol normally permits, so be it. This Nobel award changes our business profoundly. A new dawning is upon us, with the day's final results yet to be determined. Most assuredly, however, the outcome is rooted in the works of these savants.

Lest the magnitude of the event escape us, Exhibit 1 contains a complete listing of recipients of the Nobel Prize in Economic Sciences since its inception in 1969. With Markowitz, Miller, and Sharpe added to the list, the importance of financial economics is confirmed but not yet placed in perspective. To place the achievements of financial economists into a more familiar context, consider some of the Nobel Prize recipients in other arenas: Albert Einstein, Pierre and Marie Curie, Winston Churchill, Eugene O'Neil, George Bernard Shaw,

---

[1]Nobel Prizes are awarded each year on December 10 to individuals or institutions in the fields of physics, chemistry, physiology and medicine, literature, peace, and economics. Most of the prizes were established in 1901 by the will of Swedish scientist Alfred Bernhard Nobel. The Economic Sciences award was endowed in 1969 by the Bank of Sweden in memory of Nobel. The Swedish Academy of Sciences selects the recipients of this award.

[2]The task of chronicling their achievements, including the inspiration they have provided to other scholars, is awesome in the extreme. For the inevitable errors of omission and commission, I make heartfelt apologies and claim right of ownership.

Exhibit 1

Nobel Prize in Economic Sciences

Year	Winner
1969	Ragnar Frisch
	Jan Tinbergen
1970	Paul Anthony Samuelson
1971	Simon Kuznets
1972	Kenneth J. Arrow
	John R. Hicks
1973	Wassily Leontief
1974	Friedrich A. von Hayek
	Gunnar Myrdal
1975	Leonid Kantorovich
	Tjalling C. Koopmans
1976	Milton Friedman
1977	Bertil Ohlin
	James E. Meade
1978	Herbert A. Simon
1979	Theodore W. Schultz
	Sir Arthur Lewis
1980	Lawrence R. Klein
1981	James Tobin
1982	George J. Stigler
1983	Gerard Debreu
1984	Sir Richard Stone
1985	Franco Modigliani
1986	James M. Buchanan
1987	Robert Solow
1988	Maurice Allais
1989	Trygve Haavelmo
1990	Harry M. Markowitz
	Merton H. Miller
	William F. Sharpe

Rudyard Kipling, Enrico Fermi, Saul Bellow, and Mother Teresa, to name only a few. Rather auspicious, don't you think? Consider that the world can now associate "our" winners in financial economics with the intellectual heros that populate this honor roll of extraordinary individual achievement. The view is now complete: We can clearly perceive, through the company they have joined, the true stature and significance of the Markowitz–Miller–Sharpe contributions.

The story began with Markowitz's simple assumption that investors like potential return and dislike risk. These feelings are expressed through their expected utility functions. So, why not try to maximize investor utility functions? In answering this question, he proved that diversification is both smart and wise, and for the right reasons: If the utility function is maximized properly, each investor has the potential to identify the highest expected return and lowest risk combination. Markowitz also demonstrated that this goal is achieved by combining assets with expected returns that covary the least with each other. With that novel insight, he demonstrated that as one continues to combine assets into all possible portfolios, various combinations dominate others. The best collection results when, at given levels of risk, no other combinations of assets provide better expected returns; at a given level of expected return, no other asset combinations incur lower risk. The end result of that iteration process is an efficient frontier of risky portfolios.

Sharpe built on Markowitz's view of diversification and developed the capital asset pricing model (CAPM).[3] He discovered residual and systematic risks, the equilibrium conditions for asset prices, the proper descriptive and prescriptive ways to think about the world of risk and expected return trade-offs, and how to use beta to measure systematic, or nondiversifiable, risk. In short, he showed that in equilibrium, all assets are priced such that their expected returns are proportional to their risk.

Sharpe also identified the market portfolio, one of the major characteristics of which is that each asset is held in exact proportion to its market value.[4] If one desired more or less risk than that offered by the market portfolio, one could borrow or lend, buying more or less of the market portfolio.[5] In this world of equilibrium conditions, the only risk that counts is systematic risk, because all residual risk can be diversified out of the picture.

It fell to Miller and his cohort and fellow Nobel Laureate Modigliani to

---

[3]Treynor and Lintner independently explored the same territory. See: J. L. Treynor, "Toward a Theory of Market Value or Risky Assets," unpublished manuscript, 1961; and John Lintner, "The Valuation of Risk Assets and the Selection of Risk Investments in Stock Portfolios and Capital Budgets," *Review of Economics and Statistics* 47 (1965): 13–37. Arbitrage pricing theory, or APT, is another type of asset pricing model.

[4]This is the forerunner of index funds.

[5]Derivative securities now allow one to do exactly that, and much more.

show us how to value firms properly.[6] Three important ideas stem from their work: The true goal of firms should be to maximize the welfare of shareholders by maximizing their cash stream; investment decisions are independent of financing decisions; and dividend policy per se does not count for much. From this design emerges a sensible way to view the cost of capital: An opportunity cost measured as the expected return on assets of comparable risk, which can be derived from CAPM.

If shareholder welfare is to be maximized, if debt does not matter, and if dividend policy does not count for much, what market characteristics must exist for these phenomena to prevail? Enter: The efficient market hypothesis. Markets must be efficient in the sense that one cannot consistently earn abnormal returns using all known information. Prices reflect expected cash flows from a firm's investments, regardless of how they are passed on to shareholders. Share prices in an efficient market represent shareholder wealth maximization if firms undertake investments with positive net present values.

From these core concepts have spun off dozens of related theoretical advances that have fundamentally changed our perceptions of financial phenomena. We now see with new eyes such familiar constructs as diversification, dividend policy, optimal capital structure, the market portfolio, asset allocation, cost of capital, required return, and risk—both systematic and residual. "Well," you might say, "that's just about everything we do or work with." And you would be correct. It is, indeed and in deed, just about everything we do or work with.

How do the theories of Markowitz, Miller, and Sharpe fit the practitioner's milieu? Let's look. Their ideas have both conceptual implications and practical applications. One conceptual contribution lies in setting the analytical tone for subsequent generations of scholars and practitioners. For example, today we take for granted that modeling precedes analysis. At the times these three Nobelists wrote—1952, 1958, 1961, and 1964—models as we know them today were rare, almost nonexistent. Being rooted in the extant economic theory, this trio gave a distinct finance imprint to their work and set the form of procedure for all serious scholarship, whether originating in the universities or on Wall Street.

---

[6]Although the framework is corporate finance, the analytical content is universal. The intellectual predecessor is John Burr Williams, *The Theory of Investment Value* (Cambridge, Mass.: Harvard University Press, 1938).

Because of the contributions of Markowitz, Miller, and Sharpe, practitioners today reflect the ruling principles of financial economic science by analyzing problems within the models that have survived over the years. Without models, analyses usually sum to naught; they lack the fiercely demanding and necessary disciplines of deductive or inductive reasoning. Formal proofs and testable hypotheses are the order of the day. What one "thinks" does not count for much. It is what theory and evidence say that matters. Models are the engines for discovery of financial economic truths. To disregard them is to court intellectual chaos.

A second conceptual contribution of these Nobelists is that made to the ethical content of financial analysis.[7] However one may define ethical conduct, at the minimum it contains an element of giving each his due. Society's expectations of financial analysts form our ethical content: The world expects its resources to be allocated to their highest and best uses. It falls to the investment community to husband these resources based on sound theory. In making its 1990 Economic Sciences awards, the Nobel Foundation declared to the world what the accepted body of sound theory is and, in so doing, verified how investment practitioners are to comport themselves.[8]

On the applications side of the ledger, we know that the theories have been tested by time and not found wanting. The enormous array of nuts-and-bolts applications stemming from their work is impossible to chronicle in the short space available here, but they include index funds, factor models, portfolio hedging, benchmark portfolios, and poison pills. One of the most pervasive practical applications has been in the search for exceptions to the efficient market hypothesis. Armed with new knowledge and cheap computing power, researchers have been been testing a long list of possible exceptions, searching for exploitable anomalies that appear to offer rates of return in excess of those warranted by the level of risk involved. They are also looking long and hard at practitioners' traditional assumptions, methods, and results.

All of us stand a little taller in the reflected light of the Markowitz, Miller, and Sharpe achievements. Their scholarship emboldens us. We acknowledge

---

[7]For additional insights see: Association for Investment Management and Research, "The Code of Ethics and the Standards of Professional Conduct," *Standards of Practice Handbook* (Charlottesville, Va.: AIMR, 1990); and "The Ethical Content of Financial Analysis," *Financial Analysts Journal* (March/April 1991): 6.

[8]Practitioners now routinely assume responsibility for teaching, protecting, and adding to that core of theory, a responsibility that was once the province of academia.

that our stature is in large part derived from them and from the collective set of financial economists who followed them. We also know that financial economics is now on a plane that no other field of business can claim. The Markowitz–Miller–Sharpe paradigms enrich our analytical lives and our practice of asset management. They have given us a heightened sense of professional responsibility. Because they have so remarkably enhanced our professional lives, and because we build on their foundation, our debt to these three scholars is far beyond our means of payment.

The world knows us by what we do and how we do it, all of which is a product of our intellectual capital. This award sends a dramatic message: Investment professionals must continually build their intellectual capital. Failure to learn is unacceptable, as is feeding off our accumulations of knowledge. To do so dilutes our ability to make wise use of society's scarce resources.

The Research Foundation thanks AIMR for providing the resources necessary for undertaking this project. To think that AIMR's 22,000 members worldwide will have the opportunity to visit this collection of insight and innovation must surely warm the cockles of the heart. No better cause could be espoused by practitioners for practitioners.

Charles A. D'Ambrosio, CFA
Research Director
The Research Foundation of the
Institute of Chartered Financial Analysts

Foundations of Portfolio Theory

Harry M. Markowitz

Marvin Speiser Distinguished Professor of
Finance and Economics, Baruch College, CUNY,
and Director of Research, Daiwa Securities Trust Co.

When I studied microeconomics forty years ago, I was first taught how optimizing firms and consumers would behave, and then taught the nature of the economic equilibrium which would result from such behavior. Let me refer to this as part one and part two of my microeconomics course. My work on portfolio theory considers how an optimizing investor would behave, whereas the work by Sharpe and Lintner on the Capital Asset Pricing Model (CAPM for short) is concerned with economic equilibrium assuming all investors optimize in the particular manner I proposed. Thus my work on the one hand, and that of Sharpe and Lintner on the other, provide part one and part two of a microeconomics of capital markets.

Professor Sharpe will discuss CAPM, part two of the course. I will confine my remarks to part one, portfolio theory. There are three major ways in which portfolio theory differs from the theory of the firm and the theory of the consumer which I was taught. First, it is concerned with investors rather than manufacturing firms or consumers. Second, it is concerned with economic agents who act under uncertainty. Third, it is a theory which can be used to direct practice, at least by large (usually institutional) investors with sufficient computer and database resources. The fact that it deals with investors rather than producers or consumers needs no further comment. Let me expand on the second and third differences.

In my microeconomics course, the theory of the producer assumed that the competitive firm knows the price at which it will sell the goods it produces. In the real world there is a delay between the decision to produce, the time of production and the time of sale. The price of the product at the time of sale may differ from that which was expected when the production decision was made. This uncertainty of eventual sales price is important in actual production planning but, quite reasonably, was ignored in classical economic models. It was judged not essential to the problem at hand.

Uncertainty cannot be dismissed so easily in the analysis of optimizing investor behavior. An investor who knew future returns with certainty would invest in only one security, namely the one with the highest future return. If several securities had the same, highest, future return then the investor would be indifferent between any of these, or any combination of these. In no case would the investor actually prefer a diversified portfolio. But diversification is a common and reasonable investment practice. Why? To reduce uncertainty! Clearly, the existence of uncertainty is essential to the analysis of rational investment behavior.

In discussing uncertainty below, I will speak as if investors faced known probability distributions. Of course, none of us know probability distributions of security returns. But, I was convinced by Leonard J. Savage, one of my great teachers at the University of Chicago, that a rational agent acting under uncertainty would act according to "probability beliefs" where no objective probabilities are known; and these probability beliefs or "subjective probabilities" combine exactly as do objective probabilities. This assumed, it is not clear and not relevant whether the probabilities, expected values, etc., I speak of below are for subjective or objective distributions.

The basic principles of portfolio theory came to me one day while I was reading John Burr Williams, *The Theory of Investment Value*. Williams proposed that the value of a stock should equal the present value of its future dividend stream. But clearly dividends are uncertain, so I took Williams' recommendation to be to value a stock as the *expected value* of its discounted future dividend stream. But if the investor is concerned only with the expected values of securities, the investor must also be only interested in the expected value of the portfolio. To maximize the expected value of a portfolio, one need only invest in one security—the security with maximum expected return (or one such, if several tie for maximum). Thus action based on expected return only (like action based on certainty of the future) must be rejected as descriptive of actual or rational investment behavior.

It seemed obvious that investors are concerned with risk and return, and that these should be measured for the portfolio as a whole. Variance (or, equivalently, standard deviation) came to mind as a measure of risk of the portfolio. The fact that the variance of the portfolio, that is the variance of a weighted sum, involved all covariance terms added to the plausibility of the approach. Since there were two criteria—expected return and risk—the natural approach for an economics student was to imagine the investor selecting a point from the set of Pareto optimal expected return, variance of return combinations, now known as the efficient frontier. These were the basic elements of portfolio theory which appeared one day while reading Williams.

In subsequent months and years I filled in some details; and then others filled in many more. For example in 1956 I published the "critical line algorithm" for tracing out the efficient frontier given estimates of expected returns, variances and covariances, for any number of securities subject to various kinds of constraints. In my 1959 book I explored the relationship between my mean-variance analysis and the fundamental theories of action under risk and uncertainty of Von Neumann and Morgenstern and L.J. Savage.

Starting in the 1960s, Sharpe, Blume, King, Rosenberg greatly clarified the problem of estimating covariances. This past September I attended the Berkeley Program in Finance at which several analysts reported success in using publicly available accounting figures, perhaps combined with security analysts' earnings estimates, to estimate expected returns. I do not mean that their estimates eliminate uncertainty—only that, on the average, securities with higher estimates outperform those with lower estimates.

So, equipped with databases, computer algorithms and methods of estimation, the modern portfolio theorist is able to trace out mean-variance frontiers for large universes of securities. But is this the right thing to do for the investor? In particular, are mean and variance proper and sufficient criteria for portfolio choice?

To help answer this question, let us consider the theory of rational choice under uncertainty. In doing so, let us recall the third way in which portfolio theory is to differ from classical microeconomic theory of the firm or consumer. We seek a set of rules which investors can follow in fact—at least investors with sufficient computational resources. Thus we prefer an approximate method which is computationally feasible to a precise one which cannot be computed. I believe that this is the point at which Kenneth Arrow's work on the economics of uncertainty diverges from mine. He sought a precise and general solution. I sought as good an approximation as could be implemented. I believe that both lines of inquiry are valuable.

The discussion of principles of rational behavior under uncertainty in Part IV of my 1959 book starts with a variant of L.J. Savage's axioms. From such axioms it follows that one should choose a strategy which maximizes expected utility for a many-period game. This, in turn, implies that the investor should act each period so as to maximize the expected value of a single period utility function. This single period utility function may depend on portfolio return and perhaps other state variables. For now, assume that it depends only on portfolio return.

In this case, the crucial question is this: if an investor with a particular single period utility function acted only on the basis of expected return and variance, could the investor achieve almost maximum expected utility? Or, to put it another way, if you know the expected value and variance of a probability distribution of return on a portfolio can you guess fairly closely its expected utility?

A great deal of research has been done on this question, but more is needed. Let me briefly characterize some results, and some open questions. Table 1 is extracted from Levy and Markowitz. The rows of the table represent various utility functions. For example, the first row reports results for $U(R) = \log(1 + R)$ where R is the rate of return on the portfolio; the second row reports results for $U(R) = (1 + R)^{0.1}$, etc., as indicated in the first column of the table. The second through fifth columns of the table represent various sets of historical distributions of returns on portfolios. For example, the second column represents annual returns on 149 investment companies, 1958–67; the third column represents annual returns on 97 stocks, etc.

The calculations associated with the second column in effect assume that an investor must choose one out of 149 portfolios, and his probability beliefs concerning returns on these portfolios are the same as historical returns. It is not that we recommend this as a way of forming beliefs; rather, we use this as an example of distributions of returns which occur in fact.

For each utility function, and for each of the 149 probability distributions of the second column, we computed its "expected" (that is, its mean) utility

$$EU = \sum_{t=1}^{T} U(R_t)/T \tag{1}$$

where T is the number of periods in the sample, and R_t the rate of return in period t. We also computed various approximations to EU where the approximation depends only on the mean value E and the variance V of the distribution. Of the various approximations tried in Levy–Markowitz the one which did best, almost without exception, was essentially that suggested in Markowitz (1959), namely

$$f(E,V) = U(E) + .5U''(E)V \tag{2}$$

For example, if $U(R) = \log(1 + R)$,

$$f(E,V) = \log(1 + R) - .5V/(1 + E)^2. \tag{3}$$

Equation (2) may be thought of as a rule by which, if you know the E and V of a distribution, you can guess at its expected utility. The figures in Table 1 are for the Levy–Markowitz approximation which is essentially (2). The entry in the second column, first row reports that, over the 149 probability distributions, the correlation between EU and $f(E,V)$ was 0.997 for $U = \log(1 + r)$. The remaining entries in the second column similarly show the correlation, over the 149 probability distributions, of EU and $f(E,V)$ for the utility functions tested. In most cases the correlation was extremely high, usually exceeding .99. We will discuss an exceptional case shortly.

The third column shows the correlation between EU and $f(E,V)$ for a sample of annual return on one-stock "portfolios." The correlations are clearly less than for the diversified investment company portfolios of the second column. The fourth column again considers undiversified, single stock portfolios, but this time for monthly holding period returns. The correlations are much higher than those of column three, usually as high or higher than those in column two. Thus, for the investor who revises his or her portfolio monthly, even for portfolios whose returns were as variable as those of individual stocks, $f(E,V)$ would be highly correlated with EU for the utility functions considered.

The fifth column shows annual holding period returns, now for randomly selected portfolios with 5 or 6 securities each. The correlations are generally quite high again—comparable to those in the second column. Thus, at least, for these probability distributions and most of these utility functions, $f(E,V)$

Table 1

Correlation between EU and $f(E, V)$ for Four Historical Distributions

Utility Function	Annual Returns on 149 Mutual Funds[1]	Annual Returns on 97 Stocks[2]	Monthly Returns on 97 Stocks[2]	Random Portfolios of 5 or 6 Stocks[3]
$\text{Log}(1 + R)$	0.997	0.880	0.995	0.998
$(1 + R)^a$				
$a = 0.1$	0.998	0.895	0.996	0.998
$a = 0.3$	0.999	0.932	0.998	0.999
$a = 0.5$	0.999	0.968	0.999	0.999
$a = 0.7$	0.999	0.991	0.999	0.999
$a = 0.9$	0.999	0.999	0.999	0.999
$-e^{b(1+R)}$				
$b = 0.1$	0.999	0.999	0.999	0.999
$b = 0.5$	0.999	0.961	0.999	0.999
$b = 1.0$	0.997	0.850	0.997	0.998
$b = 3.0$	0.949	0.850	0.976	0.958
$b = 5.0$	0.855	0.863	0.961	0.919
$b = 10.$	0.449	0.659	0.899	0.768

1 The annual rate of return of the 149 mutual funds are taken from the various annual issues of A. Wiesenberger and Company. All mutual funds whose rates of return are reported in Wiesenberger for the whole period 1958–67 are included in the analysis.

2 This data base of 97 U.S. stocks, available at Hebrew University, had previously been obtained as follows: a sample of 100 stocks was randomly drawn from the CRSP (Center for Research in Security Prices, University of Chicago) tape, subject to the constraint that all had reported rates of return for the whole period 1948–68. Some mechanical problems reduced the usable sample size from 100 to 97. The inclusion only of stocks which had reported rates of return during the whole period may have introduced survival bias into the sample. This did not appear harmful for the purpose at hand.

3 We randomly drew 5 stocks to constitute the first portfolio; 5 different stocks to constitute the second portfolio, etc. Since we have 97 stocks in our sample, the eighteenth and nineteenth portfolios include 6 stocks each. Repetition of this experiment with new random variables produced negligible variations in the numbers reported, except for the case of $U = e^{-10(1+R)}$. A median figure is reported in the table for this case.

approximates EU quite well for diversified portfolios, even "slightly" diversified portfolios of size 5 and 6.

Not all expected utility maximizers are equally served by mean-variance approximations. For example, the investor with $U = -e^{-10(1+R)}$ will find mean-variance much less satisfactory than others presented in Table 1. Levy and Markowitz have two observations concerning an expected utility maximizer with $U = -e^{-10(1+R)}$.

The first observation is that an investor who had $-e^{-10(1+R)}$ as his or her utility function would have some very strange preferences among probabilities of return. Reasonably enough, he or she would not insist on certainty of return. For example, the investor would prefer (a) a 50–50 chance of a 5 percent gain vs. a 25 percent gain rather than have (b) a 10 percent gain with certainty. On the other hand there is no R which would induce the investor to take (a) a 50–50 chance of zero return (no gain, no loss) vs. a gain of R rather than have (b) a 10 percent return with certainty. Thus a 50–50 chance of breaking even vs. a 100,000 percent return, would be considered less desirable than a 10 percent return with certainty. We believed that few if any investors had preferences anything like these.

A second observation was that even if some unusual investor did have the utility function in question, such an investor could determine in advance that $f(E, V)$ was not a good approximation for this EU. Table 2 shows the difference between $U(R)$ and the Taylor approximation upon which (2) is based, namely,

$$Q(R) = U(E) + U'(E)(R - E) + .5U''(E)(R - E)^2 \qquad (4)$$

for $U = \log(1 + R)$ and $U = -1000e^{-10(1+R)}$, for $E = .10$. For the various R listed in the first column, the second through fourth columns show $U(R)$, $Q(R)$ and $\Delta(R) = U(R) - Q(R)$ for $\log(1 + R)$; the following three columns show the same for $-1000e^{-10(1+R)}$. Since the choices implied by a utility function are uneffected [*sic*] by multiplying it by a positive constant, it is not the magnitude of the $\Delta(R)$s which are important. Rather it is the variation in $\Delta(R)$ as compared to that in $U(R)$. For example, Levy and Markowitz present a lower bound on the correlation between $U(R)$ and $f(E,V)$ as a function of the standard deviations of U and Δ. As we see in the table, as $\log(1 + R)$ goes from $-.357$ at $R = -.30$ to $.470$ at $R = .60$, $|\Delta|$ never exceeds $.024$. In contrast, as $-1000e^{-10(1+R)}$ goes from $-.912$ to $-.0001$, $|\Delta|$ often exceeds $.03$ and has a

Table 2

Quadratic Approximation to Two Utility Functions
$E = .1$

R	$\log(1+R)$	$Q_L(R)$	Δ_L	$-1000e^{-10(1+R)}$	$Q_E(R)$	Δ_E
$-.30$	$-.35667$	$-.33444$	$-.02223$	$-.91188$	$-.21712$	$-.69476$
$-.20$	$-.22314$	$-.21461$	$-.00854$	$-.33546$	$-.14196$	$-.14950$
$-.10$	$-.10536$	$-.10304$	$-.00232$	$-.12341$	$-.08351$	$-.03990$
$.00$	$.00000$	$.00027$	$-.00027$	$-.04540$	$-.04175$	$-.00365$
$.10$	$.09531$	$.09531$	$.00000$	$-.01670$	$-.01670$	$.00000$
$.20$	$.18232$	$.18209$	$.00023$	$-.00614$	$-.00835$	$.00221$
$.30$	$.26236$	$.26060$	$.00176$	$-.00226$	$-.01670$	$.01444$
$.40$	$.33647$	$.33085$	$.00563$	$-.00083$	$-.04175$	$.04092$
$.50$	$.40546$	$.39283$	$.01263$	$-.00031$	$-.08351$	$.08320$
$.60$	$.47000$	$.44655$	$.02345$	$-.00011$	$-.14196$	$.14185$

maximum of $-.695$.[1] Thus, if an investor had $U = -e^{-10(1+R)}$ as a utility function, a comparison of $U(R)$, $Q(R)$ and $\Delta(R)$ would provide ample warning that mean-variance is not suitable.

Levy and Markowitz present other empirical results. They also explain the difference between assuming that an investor has a quadratic utility function versus using a quadratic approximation to a given utility function to develop an $f(E, V)$ approximation, such as that in (2). In particular, they show that $f(E, V)$ in (2) is not subject to the Arrow, Pratt objection to a quadratic utility function, that it has increasing risk aversion. Indeed, Levy and Markowitz show that a large class of $f(E, V)$ approximations, including (2), have the same risk aversion in the small as does the original EU maximizer.

I will not recount here these further Levy and Markowitz results, nor will I go into important results of many others. Chapter 3 of Markowitz (1987) includes a survey of the area up to that time. I will, however, briefly note results in two important unpublished papers.

Levy and Markowitz measure the efficacy of $f(E, V)$ by the correlation

---

[1] Among the 149 mutual funds, those with E near .10 all had annual returns between a 30% loss and a 60% gain. Specifically, 64 distributions had $.08 \leq E \leq .12$ and all had returns within the range indicated.

between it and EU. Y. Simaan defines the optimization premium to be the percent the investor would be just willing to pay out of the portfolio for the privilege of choosing the true EU maximizing portfolio rather than being confined to the mean-variance "second best." The reason for performing a mean-variance analysis in fact, rather than a theoretically correct expected utility analysis, is convenience, cost or feasibility. It is typically much more expensive to find a utility maximizing portfolio than to trace out an entire mean-variance frontier. The data requirements for an expected utility analysis can substantially exceed those of a mean-variance analysis, since estimates of first and second moments generally are not sufficient for the former. Finally, there is the problem of determining the investor's utility function. Simaan's criteria measures [*sic*] the worth, as a percent of the portfolio, paid out of the portfolio, of incurring the added expenses of finding an EU maximizing portfolio. He solves for this optimization premium analytically under certain assumptions.

L. Ederington evaluates EU approximations using thousands of synthetic time series generated by randomly selecting from actual times series. He evaluates approximations like (2), except that they use the first three or four moments, as well as (2) that uses the first two. It is all very well to point out theoretically that more moments are better than fewer. The practical question is: how much?

Ederington finds, as did Levy and Markowitz, that for some utility functions the mean-variance approximation is so good that there is virtually no room for improvement. Where the mean-variance approximation falters, Ederington finds that typically three moments provides little improvement to the approximation whereas four moments improves the approximation considerably.

Despite noteworthy results reported above, and many more that I have not described here, there is much to be done. Three examples will illustrate the need.

First, all the experimentation and analysis to date give us a rather spotty account of where mean-variance serves well and where it falters. Perhaps it is possible to develop a more systematic characterization of the utility functions and distributions for which the mean-variance approximation is good, bad and marginal.

Second, suppose that the investor has a utility function for which mean-variance provides a close approximation, but the investor does not know precisely what is his or her utility function. In this case the investor need not determine his or her utility function to obtain a near optimum portfolio. The investor need only pick carefully from the (one-dimensional) curve of efficient EV combinations in the two-dimensional EV space. To pursue a similar approach when four moments are required, the investor must pick carefully from a three-dimensional surface in a four-dimensional space. This raises serious operational problems in itself, even if we overcome computational problems due to the nonconvexity of sets of portfolios with given third moment or better.

But perhaps there is an alternative. Perhaps some other measure of portfolio risk will serve in a two parameter analysis for some of the utility functions which are a problem to variance. For example, in Chapter 9 of Markowitz (1959) I propose the "semi-variance" S as a measure of risk where

$$S = E(\text{Min}(0,\ R - c)^2)$$

where $c = E(R)$ or c is a constant independent of choice of portfolio. Semi-variance seems more plausible than variance as a measure of risk, since it is concerned only with adverse deviations. But, as far as I know, to date no one has determined whether there is a substantial class of utility functions for which mean-semi-variance succeeds while mean-variance fails to provide an adequate approximation to EU.

Third, in general the derived, single period utility functions can contain state-variables in addition to return (or end of period wealth). Expected utility, in this case, can be estimated from return and state-variable means, variances and covariances provided that utility is approximately quadratic in the relevant region. (Recall the Levy–Markowitz analysis of quadratic utility versus quadratic approximation in the relevant region.) To my knowledge, no one has investigated such quadratic approximation for cases in which state variables other than portfolio value are needed in practice.

In sum, it seems to me that the theory of rational behavior under uncertainty can continue to provide insights as to which practicable procedures provide near optimum results. In particular, it can further help evaluate the adequacy of mean and variance, or alternate practical measures, as criteria.

Finally, I would like to add a comment concerning portfolio theory as a part of the microeconomics of action under uncertainty. It has not always been considered so. For example, when I defended my dissertation as a student in the Economics Department of the University of Chicago, Professor Milton Friedman argued that portfolio theory was not Economics, and that they could not award me a Ph.D. degree in Economics for a dissertation which was not in Economics. I assume that he was only half serious, since they did award me the degree without long debate. As to the merits of his arguments, at this point I am quite willing to concede: at the time I defended my dissertation, portfolio theory was not part of Economics. But now it is.

References

Arrow, K. (1965), *Aspects of the Theory of Risk Bearing*, Helsinki.

Blume, M. (1971), "On the assessment of risk", *Journal of Finance*, March.

Ederington, L.H. (1986), "Mean-variance as an approximation to expected utility maximization", Working Paper 86-5, School of Business Administration, Washington University, St. Louis, Missouri.

King, B.F. (1966), "Market and industry factors in stock price behavior", *Journal of Business*, January Supplement.

Levy, H. and Markowitz, H.M. (1979), "Approximating expected utility by a function of mean and variance", *American Economic Review*, June.

Lintner, J. (1965), "The valuation of risk assets and the selection of risky investments in stock portfolios and capital budgets", *Review of Economics and Statistics*, February.

Markowitz, H.M. (1952), "Portfolio selection", *The Journal of Finance*, March.

Markowitz, H.M. (1956), "The optimization of a quadratic function subject to linear constraints", *Naval Research Logistics Quarterly*, 3.

Markowitz, H.M. (1959), *Portfolio Selection: Efficient Diversification of Investments*, Wiley, Yale University Press, 1970, Basil Blackwell, 1991.

Markowitz, H.M. (1987), Mean-Variance Analysis in Portfolio Choice and Capital Markets, Basil Blackwell, paperback edition, Basil Blackwell, 1990.

Pratt, J.W. (1964), "Risk aversion in the small and in the large", *Econometrica*.

Rosenberg, B. (1974), "Extra-market components of covariance in security returns", *Journal of Financial and Quantitative Analysis*, March.

Savage, L.J. (1954), *The Foundations of Statistics*, Wiley; 2nd ed., Dover, 1972.

Sharpe, W.F. (1963), "A simplified model for portfolio analysis", *Management Science*, January.

Sharpe, W.F. (1964), "Capital asset prices: a theory of market equilibrium under conditions of risk", *The Journal of Finance*, September.

Simaan, Y. (1987), "Portfolio selection and capital asset pricing for a class of non-spherical distributions of assets returns", dissertation, Baruch College, The City University of New York.

A. Wiesenberger and Company, *Investment Companies*, New York, annual editions.

Von Neumann, J., and Morgenstern, O. (1944), *Theory of Games and Economic Behavior*, 3rd edition, Princeton University Press, 1953.

Williams, J.B. (1938), *The Theory of Investment Value*, Harvard University Press, Cambridge, Massachusetts.

Portfolio Selection*

Harry Markowitz
The Rand Corporation

The process of selecting a portfolio may be divided into two stages. The first stage starts with observation and experience and ends with beliefs about the future performances of available securities. The second stage starts with the relevant beliefs about future performances and ends with the choice of portfolio. This paper is concerned with the second stage. We first consider the rule that the investor does (or should) maximize discounted expected, or anticipated, returns. This rule is rejected both as a hypothesis to explain, and as a maximum [*sic*] to guide investment behavior. We next consider the rule that the investor does (or should) consider expected return a desirable thing *and* variance of return an undesirable thing. This rule has many sound points, both as a maxim for, and hypothesis about, investment behavior. We illustrate geometrically relations between beliefs and choice of portfolio according to the "expected returns–variance of returns" rule.

One type of rule concerning choice of portfolio is that the investor does (or should) maximize the discounted (or capitalized) value of future returns.[1] Since the future is not known with certainty, it must be "expected" or

*This paper is based on work done by the author while at the Cowles Commission for Research in Economics and with the financial assistance of the Social Science Research Council. It will be reprinted as Cowles Commission Paper, New Series, No. 60.

[1]See, for example, J. B. Williams, *The Theory of Investment Value* (Cambridge, Mass.: Harvard University Press, 1938), pp. 55–75.

Reprinted from *The Journal of Finance* 7, (March 1952), pp. 77–91, by permission of the author and the publisher.

"anticipated" returns which we discount. Variations of this type of rule can be suggested. Following Hicks, we could let "anticipated" returns include an allowance for risk.[2] Or, we could let the rate at which we capitalize the returns from particular securities vary with risk.

The hypothesis (or maxim) that the investor does (or should) maximize discounted return must be rejected. If we ignore market imperfections the foregoing rule never implies that there is a diversified portfolio which is preferable to all non-diversified portfolios. Diversification is both observed and sensible; a rule of behavior which does not imply the superiority of diversification must be rejected both as a hypothesis and as a maxim.

The foregoing rule fails to imply diversification no matter how the anticipated returns are formed; whether the same or different discount rates are used for different securities; no matter how these discount rates are decided upon or how they vary over time.[3] The hypothesis implies that the investor places all his funds in the security with the greatest discounted value. If two or more securities have the same value, then any of these or any combination of these is as good as any other.

We can see this analytically: suppose there are N securities; let r_{it} be the anticipated return (however decided upon) at time t per dollar invested in security i; let d_{it} be the rate at which the return on the ith security at time t is discounted back to the present; let X_i be the relative amount invested in security i. We exclude short sales, thus $X_i \geq 0$ for all i. Then the discounted anticipated return of the portfolio is

$$R = \sum_{t=1}^{\infty} \sum_{i=1}^{N} d_{it} r_{it} X$$

$$= \sum_{i=1}^{N} X_i \left(\sum_{t=1}^{\infty} d_{it} r_{it} \right)$$

---

[2]J. R. Hicks, *Value and Capital* (New York: Oxford University Press, 1939), p. 126. Hicks applies the rule to a firm rather than a portfolio.

[3]The results depend on the assumption that the anticipated returns and discount rates are independent of the particular investor's portfolio.

$$R_i = \sum_{t=1}^{\infty} d_{it} r_{it} \quad \text{is the discounted return of the } i^{th} \text{ security, therefore}$$

$R = \Sigma X_i R_i$ where R_i is independent of X_i. Since $X_i \geq 0$ for all i and $\Sigma X_i = 1$, R is a weighted average of R_i with the X_i as non-negative weights. To maximize R, we let $X_i = 1$ for i with maximum R_i. If several Ra_a, $a = 1, \ldots, K$ are maximum then any allocation with

$$\sum_{a=1}^{K} Xa_a = 1$$

maximizes R. In no case is a diversified portfolio preferred to all non-diversified portfolios. [4]

It will be convenient at this point to consider a static model. Instead of speaking of the time series of returns from the ith security ($r_{i1}, r_{i2}, \ldots, r_{it}, \ldots$) we will speak of "the flow of returns" (r_i) from the ith security. The flow of returns from the portfolio as a whole is $R = \Sigma X_i r_i$. As in the dynamic case if the investor wished to maximize "anticipated" returns from the portfolio he would place all his funds in that security with maximum anticipated returns.

There is a rule which implies both that the investor should diversify and that he should maximize expected return. The rule states that the investor does (or should) diversify his funds among all those securities which give maximum expected return. The law of large numbers will insure that the actual yield of the portfolio will be almost the same as the expected yield. [5] This rule is a special case of the expected returns–variance of returns rule (to be presented below). It assumes that there is a portfolio which gives both maximum expected return and minimum variance, and it commends this portfolio to the investor.

This presumption, that the law of large numbers applies to a portfolio of securities, cannot be accepted. The returns from securities are too intercorrelated. Diversification cannot eliminate all variance.

The portfolio with maximum expected return is not necessarily the one

---

[4] If short sales were allowed, an infinite amount of money would be placed in the security with highest r.

[5] Williams, *op. cit.*, pp. 68, 69.

with minimum variance. There is a rate at which the investor can gain expected return by taking on variance, or reduce variance by giving up expected return.

We saw that the expected returns or anticipated returns rule is inadequate. Let us now consider the expected returns–variance of returns (E–V) rule. It will be necessary to first present a few elementary concepts and results of mathematical statistics. We will then show some implications of the E–V rule. After this we will discuss its plausibility.

In our presentation we try to avoid complicated mathematical statements and proofs. As a consequence a price is paid in terms of rigor and generality. The chief limitations from this source are (1) we do not derive our results analytically for the n-security case; instead, we present them geometrically for the 3 and 4 security cases; (2) we assume static probability beliefs. In a general presentation we must recognize that the probability distribution of yields of the various securities is a function of time. The writer intends to present, in the future, the general, mathematical treatment which removes these limitations.

We will need the following elementary concepts and results of mathematical statistics:

Let Y be a random variable, i.e., a variable whose value is decided by chance. Suppose, for simplicity of exposition, that Y can take on a finite number of values $y_1, y_2, \ldots, y_N$. Let the probability that $Y = y_1$, be p_1; that $Y = y_2$ be p_2 etc. The expected value (or mean) of Y is defined to be

$$E = p_1 y_1 + p_2 y_2 + \cdots + p_N y_N$$

The variance of Y is defined to be

$$V = p_1(y_1 - E)^2 + p_2(y_2 - E)^2 + \cdots + p_N (y_N - E)^2.$$

V is the average squared deviation of Y from its expected value. V is a commonly used measure of dispersion. Other measures of dispersion, closely related to V are the standard deviation, $\sigma = \sqrt{V}$ and the coefficient of variation, σ/E.

Suppose we have a number of random variables: $R_1, \ldots, R_n$. If R is a weighted sum (linear combination) of the R_i

$$R = a_1 R_1 + a_2 R_2 + \cdots + a_n R_n$$

then R is also a random variable. (For example R_1, may be the number which turns up on one die; R_2, that of another die, and R the sum of these numbers. In this case $n = 2$, $a_1 = a_2 = 1$).

It will be important for us to know how the expected value and variance of the weighted sum (R) are related to the probability distribution of the $R_1, \ldots, R_n$. We state these relations below; we refer the reader to any standard text for proof. [6]

The expected value of a weighted sum is the weighted sum of the expected values. I.e., $E(R) = a_1 E(R_1) + a_2 E(R_2) + \cdots + a_n E(R_n)$. The variance of a weighted sum is not as simple. To express it we must define "covariance." The covariance of R_1 and R_2 is

$$\sigma_{12} = E\{[R_1 - E(R_1)][R_2 - E(R_2)]\}$$

i.e., the expected value of [(the deviation of R_1 from its mean) times (the deviation of R_2 from its mean)]. In general we define the covariance between R_i and R_j as

$$\sigma_{ij} = E\{[R_i - E(R_i)][R_i - E(R_j)]\}$$

σ_{ij} may be expressed in terms of the familiar correlation coefficient (ρ_{ij}). The covariance between R_i and R_j is equal to [(their correlation) times (the standard deviation of R_i) times (the standard deviation of R_j)]:

$$\sigma_{ij} = \rho_{ij}\sigma_i\sigma_j$$

The variance of a weighted sum is

$$V(R) = \sum_{i=1}^{N} a_i^2 V(X_i) + 2 \sum_{i=1}^{N} \sum_{i>1}^{N} a_i a_j \sigma_{ij}$$

If we use the fact that the variance of R_i is σ_{ii} then

$$V(R) = \sum_{i=1}^{N} \sum_{j=1}^{N} a_i a_j \sigma_{ij}$$

Let R_i be the return on the ith security. Let μ_i be the expected value of R_i; σ_{ij}, be the covariance between R_i and R_j (thus σ_{ii} is the variance of R_i). Let X_i be the percentage of the investor's assets which are allocated to the ith security. The yield (R) on the portfolio as a whole is

---

[6]E.g., J. V. Uspensky, *Introduction to Mathematical Probability* (New York: McGraw–Hill, 1937), chapter 9, pp. 161–81.

$$R = \sum R_i X_i$$

The R_i (and consequently R) are considered to be random variables. [7] The X_i are not random variables, but are fixed by the investor. Since the X_i are percentages we have $\Sigma X_i = 1$. In our analysis we will exclude negative values of the X_i (i.e., short sales); therefore $X_i \geq 0$ for all i.

The return (R) on the portfolio as a whole is a weighted sum of random variables (where the investor can choose the weights). From our discussion of such weighted sums we see that the expected return E from the portfolio as a whole is

$$E = \sum_{i=1}^{N} X_i \mu_i$$

and the variance is

$$V = \sum_{i=1}^{N} \sum_{j=1}^{N} \sigma_{ij} X_i X$$

For fixed probability beliefs (μ_i, σ_{ij}) the investor has a choice of various combinations of E and V depending on his choice of portfolio $X_1, \ldots, X_N$. Suppose that the set of all obtainable (E, V) combinations were as in Figure 1. The E–V rule states that the investor would (or should) want to select one of those portfolios which give rise to the (E, V) combinations indicated as efficient in the figure; i.e., those with minimum V for given E or more and maximum E for given V or less.

There are techniques by which we can compute the set of efficient portfolios and efficient (E, V) combinations associated with given μ_i and σ_{ij}. We will not present these techniques here. We will, however, illustrate geometri-

---

[7]I.e., we assume that the investor does (and should) act as if he had probability beliefs concerning these variables. In general we would expect that the investor could tell us, for any two events (A and B), whether he personally considered A more likely than B, B more likely than A, or both equally likely. If the investor were consistent in his opinions on such matters, he would possess a system of probability beliefs. We cannot expect the investor to be consistent in every detail. We can, however, expect his probability beliefs to be roughly consistent on important matters that have been carefully considered. We should also expect that he will base his actions upon these probability beliefs—even though they be in part subjective.

This paper does not consider the difficult question of how investors do (or should) form their probability beliefs.

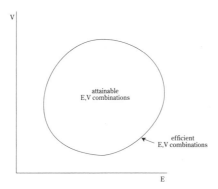

Figure 1

cally the nature of the efficient surfaces for cases in which N (the number of available securities) is small.

The calculation of efficient surfaces might possibly be of practical use. Perhaps there are ways, by combining statistical techniques and the judgment of experts, to form reasonable probability beliefs (μ_i, σ_{ij}). We could use these beliefs to compute the attainable efficient combinations of (E, V). The investor, being informed of what (E, V) combinations were attainable, could state which he desired. We could then find the portfolio which gave this desired combination.

Two conditions—at least—must be satisfied before it would be practical to use efficient surfaces in the manner described above. First, the investor must desire to act according to the E–V maxim. Second, we must be able to arrive at reasonable μ_i and σ_{ij}. We will return to these matters later.

Let us consider the case of three securities. In the three security case our model reduces to

1) $E = \displaystyle\sum_{i=1}^{3} X_i \mu_i$

2) $V = \displaystyle\sum_{i=1}^{3} \sum_{j=1}^{3} X_i X_j \sigma_{ij}$

3) $\displaystyle\sum_{i=1}^{3} X_i = 1$

19

4) $X_i \geq 0$ for $i = 1, 2, 3$.

From (3) we get

3') $X_3 = 1 - X_1 - X_2$

If we substitute (3') in equation (1) and (2) we get E and V as functions of X_1 and X_2. For example we find

1') $E = \mu_3 + X_1(\mu_1 - \mu_3) + X_2(\mu_2 - \mu_3)$

The exact formulas are not too important here (that of V is given below). [8] We can simply write

   a) $E = E(X_1, X_2)$

   b) $V = V(X_1, X_2)$

   c) $X_1 \geq 0, X_2 \geq 0, 1 - X_1 - X_2 \geq 0$

By using relations (*a*), (*b*), (*c*), we can work with two dimensional geometry.

The attainable set of portfolios consists of all portfolios which satisfy constraints (*c*) and (3') (or equivalently (3) and (4)). The attainable combinations of X_1, X_2 are represented by the triangle $\overline{abc}$ in Figure 2. Any point to the left of the X_2 axis is not attainable because it violates the condition that $X_1 \geq 0$. Any point below the X_1 axis is not attainable because it violates the condition that $X_2 \geq 0$. Any point above the line $(1 - X_1 - X_2 = 0)$ is not attainable because it violates the condition that $X_3 = 1 - X_1 - X_2 \geq 0$.

We define an *isomean* curve to be the set of all points (portfolios) with a given expected return. Similarly an *isovariance* line is defined to be the set of all points (portfolios) with a given variance of return.

An examination of the formulae for E and V tells us the shapes of the isomean and isovariance curves. Specifically they tell us that typically[9] the isomean curves are a system of parallel straight lines; the isovariance curves

---

[8] $V = X_1^2(\sigma_{11} - 2\sigma_{13} + \sigma_{33}) + X_2^2(\sigma_{22} - 2\sigma_{23} + \sigma_{33}) + 2X_1X_2(\sigma_{12} - \sigma_{13} - \sigma_{23} + \sigma_{33}) + 2X_1(\sigma_{12} - \sigma_{33}) + 2X_2(\sigma_{23} - \sigma_{33}) + \sigma_{33}$

[9] The isomean "curves" are as described above except when $\mu_1 = \mu_2 = \mu_3$. In the latter case all portfolios have the same expected return and the investor chooses the one with minimum variance.

As to the assumptions implicit in our description of the isovariance curves see footnote 12.

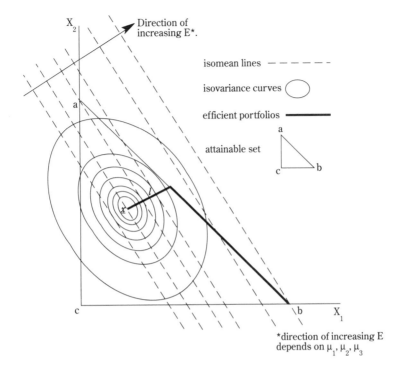

Figure 2

are a system of concentric ellipses (see Fig. 2). For example, if $\mu_2 \neq \mu_3$ equation 1′ can be written in the familiar form $X_2 = a + bX_1$; specifically (1)

$$X_2 = \frac{E - \mu_3}{\mu_2 - \mu_3} - \frac{\mu_1 - \mu_3}{\mu_2 - \mu_3} X_1.$$

Thus the slope of the isomean line associated with $E = E_0$ is $-(\mu_1 - \mu_3)/(\mu_2 - \mu_3)$ its intercept is $(E_0 - \mu_3)/(\mu_2 - \mu_3)$. If we change E we change the intercept but not the slope of the isomean line. This confirms the contention that the isomean lines form a system of parallel lines.

Similarly, by a somewhat less simple application of analytic geometry, we can confirm the contention that the isovariance lines form a family of concentric ellipses. The "center" of the system is the point which minimizes V. We will label this point X. Its expected return and variance we will label E and V. Variance increases as you move away from X. More precisely, if one isovariance curve, C_1, lies closer to X than another, C_2, then C_1 is associated with a smaller variance than C_2.

With the aid of the foregoing geometric apparatus let us seek the efficient sets.

X, the center of the system of isovariance ellipses, may fall either inside or outside the attainable set. Figure 4 illustrates a case in which X falls inside the attainable set. In this case: X is efficient. For no other portfolio has a V as low as X; therefore no portfolio can have either smaller V (with the same or greater E) or greater E with the same or smaller V. No point (portfolio) with expected return E less than E is efficient. For we have $E > E$ and $V < V$.

Consider all points with a given expected return E; i.e., all points on the isomean line associated with E. The point of the isomean line at which V takes on its least value is the point at which the isomean line is tangent to an isovariance curve. We call this point $\hat{X}(E)$. If we let E vary, $\hat{X}(E)$ traces out a curve.

Algebraic considerations (which we omit here) show us that this curve is a straight line. We will call it the critical line l. The critical line passes through X for this point minimizes V for all points with $E(X_1, X_2) = E$. As we go along l in either direction from X, V increases. The segment of the critical line from X to the point where the critical line crosses the boundary of the attainable set is part of the efficient set. The rest of the efficient set is (in the case illustrated) the segment of the $\overline{ab}$ line from d to b. b is the point of maximum attainable E. In Figure 3, X lies outside the admissible area but the critical line cuts the admissible area. The efficient line begins at the attainable point with minimum variance (in this case on the $\overline{ab}$ line). It moves toward b until it intersects the critical line, moves along the critical line until it intersects a boundary and finally moves along the boundary to b. The reader may wish to construct and examine the following other cases: (1) X lies outside the attainable set and the critical line does not cut the attainable set. In this case there is a security which does not enter into any efficient portfolio. (2) Two securities have the same μ_i. In this case the isomean lines are parallel to a boundary line. It may happen that the efficient portfolio with maximum E is a diversified portfolio. (3) A case wherein only one portfolio is efficient.

The efficient set in the 4 security case is, as in the 3 security and also the N security case, a series of connected line segments. At one end of the efficient

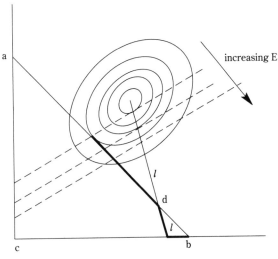

Figure 3

set is the point of minimum variance; at the other end is a point of maximum expected return[10] (see Fig. 4).

Now that we have seen the nature of the set of efficient portfolios, it is not difficult to see the nature of the set of efficient (E, V) combinations. In the three security case $E = a_0 + a_1X_1 + a_2X_2$ is a plane; $V = b_0 + b_1X_1 + b_2X_2 + b_{12}X_1X_2 + b_{11}X_1^2 + b_{22}X_2^2$ is a paraboloid.[11] As shown in Figure 5, the section of the E-plane over the efficient portfolio set is a series of connected

---

[10]Just as we used the equation $\sum_{i=1}^{4} X_i = 1$ to reduce the dimensionality in the three security case, we can use it to represent the four security case in 3 dimensional space. Eliminating X_4 we get $E = E(X_1, X_2, X_3)$, $V = V(X_1, X_2, X_3)$. The attainable set is represented, in three-space, by the tetrahedron with vertices (0, 0, 0), (0, 0, 1), (0, 1, 0), (1, 0, 0), representing portfolios with, respectively, $X_4 = 1$, $X_3 = 1$, $X_2 = 1$, $X_1 = 1$.

Let s_{123} be the subspace consisting of all points with $X_4 = 0$. Similarly we can define $s_{a1}, \ldots, a_a$ to be the subspace consisting of all points with $X_i = 0$, $i \neq a_1, \ldots, a_a$. For each subspace $s_{a1}, \ldots, a_a$ we can define a *critical line* $la_1, \ldots, a_a$. This line is the locus of points P where P minimizes V for all points in $s_{a1}, \ldots, a_a$ with the same E as P. If a point is in $s_{a1}, \ldots, a_a$ and is efficient it must be on $la_1, \ldots, a_a$. The efficient set may be traced out by starting at the point of minimum available variance, moving continuously along various $la_1, \ldots, a_a$ according to definite rules, ending in a point which gives maximum E. As in the two dimensional case the point with minimum available variance may be in the interior of the available set or on one of its boundaries. Typically we proceed along a given critical line until either this line intersects one of a larger subspace or meets a boundary (and simultaneously the critical line of a lower dimensional subspace). In either of these cases the efficient line turns and continues along the new line. The efficient line terminates when a point with maximum E is reached.

[11]See footnote 8.

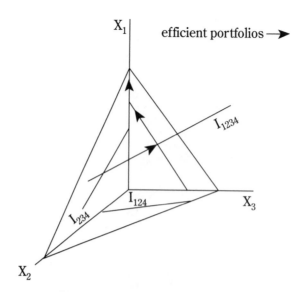

Figure 4

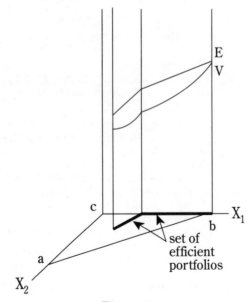

Figure 5

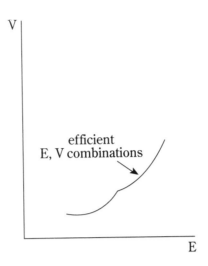

Figure 6

line segments. The section of the *V*-paraboloid over the efficient portfolio set is a series of connected parabola segments. If we plotted *V* against *E* for efficient portfolios we would again get a series of connected parabola segments (see Fig. 6). This result obtains for any number of securities.

    Various reasons recommend the use of the expected return–variance of return rule, both as a hypothesis to explain well-established investment behavior and as a maxim to guide one's own action. The rule serves better, we will see, as an explanation of, and guide to, "investment" as distinguished from "speculative" behavior.

    Earlier we rejected the expected returns rule on the grounds that it never implied the superiority of diversification. The expected return–variance of return rule, on the other hand, implies diversification for a wide range of μ_i, σ_{ij}. This does not mean that the *E*–*V* rule never implies the superiority of an undiversified portfolio. It is conceivable that one security might have an extremely higher yield and lower variance than all other securities; so much so that one particular undiversified portfolio would give maximum *E* and minimum *V*. But for a large, presumably representative range of μ_i, σ_{ij} the *E*–*V* rule leads to efficient portfolios almost all of which are diversified.

    Not only does the *E*–*V* hypothesis imply diversification, it implies the "right kind" of diversification for the "right reason." The adequacy of diversification is not thought by investors to depend solely on the number of different securities held. A portfolio with sixty different railway securities, for example, would not be as well diversified as the same size portfolio with some railroad, some public utility, mining, various sort of manufacturing, etc. The reason is that it is generally more likely for firms within the same industry to do poorly at the same time than for firms in dissimilar industries.

Similarly in trying to make variance small it is not enough to invest in many securities. It is necessary to avoid investing in securities with high covariances among themselves. We should diversify across industries because firms in different industries, especially industries with different economic characteristics, have lower covariances than firms within an industry.

The concepts "yield" and "risk" appear frequently in financial writings. Usually if the term "yield" were replaced by "expected yield" or "expected return," and "risk" by "variance of return," little change of apparent meaning would result.

Variance is a well-known measure of dispersion about the expected. If instead of variance the investor was concerned with standard error, $\sigma = \sqrt{V}$, or with the coefficient of dispersion, σ/E, his choice would still lie in the set of efficient portfolios.

Suppose an investor diversifies between two portfolios (i.e., if he puts some of his money in one portfolio, the rest of his money in the other. An example of diversifying among portfolios is the buying of the shares of two different investment companies). If the two original portfolios have *equal* variance then typically[12] the variance of the resulting (compound) portfolio will be less than the variance of either original portfolio. This is illustrated by Figure 7. To interpret Figure 7 we note that a portfolio (P) which is built out of two portfolios $P' = (X_1', X_2')$ and $P'' = (X_1'', X_2'')$ is of the form $P = \lambda P' + (1 - \lambda)P'' = (\lambda X_1' + (1 - \lambda)X_1'', \lambda X_2' + (1 - \lambda)X_2'')$. P is on the straight line connecting P' and P''.

The E–V principle is more plausible as a rule for investment behavior as distinguished from speculative behavior. The third moment[13] M_3 of the

---

[12]In no case will variance be increased. The only case in which variance will not be decreased is if the return from both portfolios are perfectly correlated. To draw the isovariance curves as ellipses it is both necessary and sufficient to assume that no two distinct portfolios have perfectly correlated returns.

[13]If R is a random variable that takes on a finite number of values $r_1, \ldots, r_n$ with probabilities $p_1, \ldots, p_n$ respectively, and expected value E,

$$\text{then } M_3 = \sum_{i=1}^{n} p_i(r_i - E)^3$$

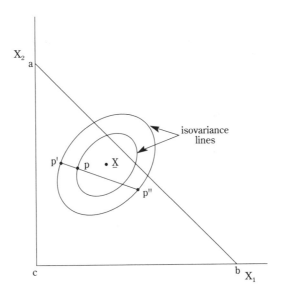

Figure 7

probability distribution of returns from the portfolio may be connected with a propensity to gamble. For example if the investor maximizes utility (U) which depends on E and $V(U = U(E, V), \partial U/\partial E > 0, \partial U/\partial E < 0)$ he will never accept an actuarially fair[14] bet. But if $U = U(E, V, M_3)$ and if $\partial U/\partial M_3 \neq 0$ then there are some fair bets which would be accepted.

Perhaps—for a great variety of investing institutions which consider yield to be a good thing; risk, a bad thing; gambling, to be avoided—E, V efficiency is reasonable as a working hypothesis and a working maxim.

Two uses of the E–V principle suggest themselves. We might use it in theoretical analyses or we might use it in the actual selection of portfolios.

In theoretical analyses we might inquire, for example, about the various effects of a change in the beliefs generally held about a firm, or a general change in preference as to expected return versus variance of return, or a change in the supply of a security. In our analyses the X_i might represent individual securities

---

[14] One in which the amount gained by winning the bet times the probability of winning is equal to the amount lost by losing the bet, times the probability of losing.

or they might represent aggregates such as, say, bonds, stocks and real estate. [15]

To use the E–V rule in the selection of securities we must have procedures for finding reasonable μ_i and σ_{ij}. These procedures, I believe, should combine statistical techniques and the judgment of practical men. My feeling is that the statistical computations should be used to arrive at a tentative set of μ_i and σ_{ij}. Judgment should then be used in increasing or decreasing some of these μ_i and σ_{ij} on the basis of factors or nuances not taken into account by the formal computations. Using this revised set of μ_i and σ_{ij}, the set of efficient E, V combinations could be computed, the investor could select the combination he preferred, and the portfolio which gave rise to this E, V combination could be found.

One suggestion as to tentative μ_i, σ_{ij} is to use the observed μ_i, σ_{ij} for some period of the past. I believe that better methods, which take into account more information, can be found. I believe that what is needed is essentially a "probabilistic" reformulation of security analysis. I will not pursue this subject here, for this is "another story." It is a story of which I have read only the first page of the first chapter.

In this paper we have considered the second stage in the process of selecting a portfolio. This stage starts with the relevant beliefs about the securities involved and ends with the selection of a portfolio. We have not considered the first stage: the formation of the relevant beliefs on the basis of observation.

---

[15]Care must be used in using and interpreting relations among aggregates. We cannot deal here with the problems and pitfalls of aggregation.

Nobel Lecture

December 7, 1990

Capital Asset Prices with and without Negative Holdings

William F. Sharpe*

Timken Professor Emeritus of Finance
Stanford University Graduate School of Business
Chairman, William F. Sharpe Associates

Introduction

Following tradition, I deal here with the Capital Asset Pricing Model, a subject with which I have been associated for over 25 years, and which the Royal Swedish Academy of Sciences has cited in honoring me with the award of the Prize in Economic Sciences in Memory of Alfred Nobel.

I first present the Capital Asset Pricing Model (hence, CAPM), incorporating not only my own contributions[1] but also the outstanding work of Lintner (1965, 1969) and the contributions of Mossin (1966) and others. My goal is to do so succinctly yet in a manner designed to emphasize the economic content of the theory.

*I am particularly grateful for the detailed comments and suggestions on the contents of this lecture provided by Robert Litzenberger and André Perold. Subsequent comments and suggestions by Haim Levy and Harry Markowitz are also gratefully acknowledged. My longer-term debt to colleagues in many places is also substantial; I particularly wish to thank those at Stanford University and at William F. Sharpe Associates for their contributions to my work over the years.

[1] beginning with Sharpe (1961) and Sharpe (1964).

Following this, I modify the model to reflect an extreme case of an institutional arrangement that can preclude investors from choosing fully optimal portfolios. In particular, I assume that investors are unable to take negative positions in assets. For this version of the model I draw heavily from papers by Glenn (1976), Levy (1978), Merton (1987) and Markowitz (1987, 1990).

Finally, I discuss the stock index futures contract—a major financial innovation of worldwide importance that postdates the development of the CAPM. Such contracts can increase the efficiency of capital markets in many ways. In particular, they can bring actual markets closer to the idealized world assumed by the Capital Asset Pricing Model.

The Capital Asset Pricing Model

The initial version of the CAPM, developed over 25 years ago, was extremely parsimonious. It dealt with the central aspects of equilibrium in capital markets and assumed away many important aspects of such markets as they existed at the time. In the last 25 years, theorists have extended and adapted the approach to incorporate some of these real-world phenomena. Important examples are Lintner's (1969) version, which focuses on returns in real terms; Brennan's (1970) version, which deals with the effects of taxation; Black's (1972) version, in which there is no riskless asset; Merton's (1973) version, which incorporates investors' concern with future investment opportunities; Rubinstein's (1974) version, which deals with a more general class of utility functions; Kraus and Litzenberger's (1976) version, which takes into account the third moment of the return distribution; Levy's (1978) version, which incorporates transactions costs; Breeden's (1979) version, which focuses on investors' preferences for consumption; Merton's (1987) version, which deals with market segmentation; and Markowitz' (1990) version, which considers restrictions on short sales.

Throughout, empiricists have subjected variations of the model to tests of increasing power. Moreover, alternative methods have been proposed, most notably Ross' (1976) Arbitrage Pricing Theory.

While theorists have been busy adapting the CAPM to incorporate real-world impediments to efficiency, practitioners have been equally busy reducing some of those impediments. Many of the financial instruments and institutions developed in the last decade serve to better "complete the markets"—in particular, to allow a more efficient distribution of risk among investors.

I will not attempt a general treatment of the institutional costs and constraints that can affect the efficiency with which risk is allocated, nor of the many recent financial innovations that serve to reduce such costs and constraints. Instead, I will focus on one prototypical example—restrictions on negative positions in securities, and one such innovation—stock index futures.

To facilitate the exposition, many formulas and proofs will be relegated to footnotes. In this I follow a long personal tradition, since a key proof in Sharpe (1964)—my first published paper on the Capital Asset Pricing Model—was contained in a footnote. [2]

The CAPM and Financial Economic Theory

A common taxonomy of work in financial economics differentiates between *normative* (prescriptive) and *positive* (descriptive) theories. Markowitz' (1952) path-breaking mean-variance portfolio theory falls cleanly into the former category, dealing as it does with rules for optimal portfolio choice by an individual. The CAPM can be neatly classified as belonging to the latter, since it is concerned with the determination of the prices of capital assets in a competitive market. But two such categories are not sufficient. Much of the work in the field can best be described as approaching *normative issues in a positive context*. The seminal Modigliani–Miller (1958) model is of this genre, since it prescribes optimal behavior for a corporation faced with a capital market in which security prices are determined by the actions of individual investors cognizant of opportunities for substitution.

Even this three-way taxonomy fails to capture the interrelationships among the alternative approaches. Most positive models in financial economics, like those in the broader field of economics, are built on normative foundations. Individuals engaging in maximizing behavior are assumed to interact with one another until an equilibrium condition is reached. This is clearly the case with the CAPM, which explicitly assumes that investors follow the prescriptions of Markowitz' portfolio theory. Moreover, as in traditional micro-economic theory, financial economic theories of equilibrium relationships are taken as prescriptions for decisions in markets that may not strictly conform to the conditions of the theory.

The domain of positive financial economics theory is sometimes divided

---

[2] more specifically, footnote 22.

into a set of models that may be termed *utility-based* and a complementary set that may be termed *arbitrage-based*. Models that fall in the latter category derive implications from the assumption that capital asset prices will adjust until it is impossible to find a strategy that requires no initial investment, provides a positive cash flow in at least one state of nature, and requires no negative cash flow in any future state of nature.[3] Models that fall in the former category typically conform to the conditions required for the latter, but derive stronger implications due to added assumptions about the *utility functions* that investors are assumed to maximize.[4]

Much of the early work in financial economics dealt with markets in which the interaction of a large number of individuals, each equally informed, determined prices. In this sense the work followed the tradition of competitive equilibrium theory in economics. More recently, attention has focused on markets in which there are few participants and/or in which different individuals have different sets of information.

The CAPM is, of course, a theory in the earlier tradition of the field. It is a positive theory, incorporates assumptions about investors' utility functions, and assumes a market with a large number of participants, each of whom has access to the same set of information.

Capital Asset Prices with Negative Holdings

Assumptions

Assume that the economy consists of K investors. Investor k's invested wealth, expressed as a proportion of the total wealth invested by all investors, is W_k. He or she wishes to maximize:

---

[3]Prominent arbitrage-based theories in financial economics are the Black–Scholes (1973) model, which deals with the prices of options vis-a-vis related securities, and Ross' (1976) Arbitrage Pricing Theory, which draws implications about the prices of capital assets when returns are generated by a specified factor model. While the monumental Arrow (1953) Debreu (1959) state-preference approach to uncertainty makes some assumptions about individual's utility functions, many of its key results are arbitrage-based. A number of theories in financial economics have been constructed using the Arrow–Debreu "state of the world" paradigm, among them the binomial model of option pricing first presented in my textbook (1978) and then extended by Cox, Ross, and Rubinstein (1979) and many others.

[4]It is, of course, true that arbitrage-based models make some assumptions about investor preferences—for example, that investors prefer larger payoffs to smaller payoffs in any given state of the world. However, such assumptions are minimal, compared with the more detailed assumptions of utility-based models.

$$U_k = E_k - \frac{V_k}{\tau_k}. \tag{1}$$

For expository convenience, I will term U_k investor k's *utility*. It may be regarded as a primitive utility function. Alternatively, it may be considered an approximation to the investor's *expected utility* in the sense of Von Neumann and Morgenstern (1944). If the investor is assumed to have a negative exponential utility function over wealth and returns are jointly normally distributed, the approximation will be exact. Even if the investor has some other utility function and/or returns are not jointly normally distributed, U_k may provide an excellent approximation, as shown by Levy and Markowitz (1979).

In equation (1), E_k is the expected return on investor k's portfolio, V_k is the variance of the portfolio, and τ_k is his or her risk tolerance. Investors differ in risk tolerance.

This relationship can be interpreted in a number of useful ways. Clearly, risk tolerance measures an investor's *marginal rate of substitution of variance for expected return*. For convenience we assume that each investor's risk tolerance is constant over the feasible range of expected return and variance.[5]

The value obtained by dividing portfolio variance by an investor's risk tolerance can be characterized as a *risk penalty*, leading to the interpretation of U_k as a *risk-adjusted expected return*. Alternatively, U_k may be considered a *certainty-equivalent* return, since a portfolio with a return of U_k and zero risk would have the same utility for the investor as the portfolio in question.

This is the objective function of Markowitz' (1952) "mean-variance" approach to portfolio selection. It is a highly parsimonious characterization of investors' goals, employing a myopic view (i.e. "one period at a time") and focusing on only two aspects of the probability distribution of possible returns over that period.[6] Moreover, it assumes that the investor[7] can assess at least the first two moments of the probability distributions associated with alternative

---

[5]This is not required. The results that follow can be obtained under more general conditions, with the resultant values of τ_k interpreted as investors' marginal rates of substitution, given their optimal holdings.

[6]Note, however, that this assumption will be less onerous, the shorter the time period under consideration. In continuous-time versions of the model, the time period is (in effect) infinitesimal in length. Under such conditions, two moments may serve as adequate representations even if the probability distribution of returns over a finite period and/or investors' preferences for returns over such a period are quite complex.

[7]aided, perhaps by an advisor

investment portfolios. The genius of the approach is its ability to capture much of what matters to investors. Moreover, it serves well as a base for extensions and adaptations designed to accommodate additional aspects of investors' preferences.

As in Markowitz' work, the expected return on a portfolio depends on the expected returns on its component securities. [8] A portfolio's risk depends on both the risks of the component securities and on their correlations with one another. More succinctly: portfolio risk depends on the covariances among securities. [9]

All investors are in agreement concerning expected returns and covariances. Of course, these moments of the joint distribution of security returns will be a function of security prices. When equilibrium prices are attained, however, each investor will choose an optimal portfolio, given the current values of expected returns and covariances; moreover the resultant portfolio choices will cause the markets to clear.

Investors are allowed to take negative positions in one or more assets. Thus holdings may be positive, zero or negative. There are no transactions costs or other constraints and asset positions are fully divisible.

Portfolio Optimality

Investor k seeks to maximize U_k subject to a *full investment constraint* of the form:

$$\sum_i X_{ik} = 1.$$

where X_{ik} represents the proportion of investor k's portfolio invested in asset i.

To do so, he or she must select a portfolio in which the *marginal utility*

---

[8]The expected return of investor k's portfolio is given by:

$$E_k = \sum_i X_{ik} E_i$$

where X_{ik} represents the proportion of investor k's portfolio invested in asset i.

[9]The variance of investor k's portfolio is given by:

$$V_k = \sum_i \sum_j X_{ik} X_{jk} C_{ij}$$

where C_{ij} represents the covariance between the returns on assets i and j.

of every security is the same. If this were not the case, it would be possible to reallocate funds from a security with a lower marginal utility to one with a higher one, thereby increasing utility without violating the full investment constraint.

This *first order condition* for portfolio optimality can be represented as follows:

$$E_i - \frac{2}{\tau_k} C_{ik} = \lambda_{fk} \quad \text{for all i.} \tag{2}$$

Here C_{ik} is the covariance of security i with investor k's optimal portfolio and λ_{fk} is investor k's *marginal utility of wealth.* [10]

Aggregation

Assume that markets have cleared, so that all securities are held by the K investors in the economy. Relationships among key variables can be examined by aggregating the conditions that must hold when each investor obtains an optimal solution, taking into account the relative amounts of wealth that each

---

[10]Incorporating U_k and the full investment constraint in a Lagrangean function to be maximized gives:

$$Z_k = U_k + \lambda_{fk}\left(1 - \sum_i X_{ik}\right).$$

Clearly λ_{fk} is *marginal utility of wealth* for investor k, since it equals the partial derivative of Z_k with respect to the investor's wealth (in this metric, the value 1 in the parenthesized full investment constraint, since the X_{ik} values are expressed as proportions of the investor's total wealth). Recall that:

$$E_k = \sum_k X_{ik}E_i, \quad \text{and}$$

$$V_k = \sum_i \sum_j X_{ik} X_{jk} C_{ij}.$$

Hence, taking the partial derivative of Z_k with respect to investor k's holding of security i gives:

$$\frac{\partial Z_k}{\partial X_{ik}} = E_i - \frac{2}{\tau_k} \sum_j X_{jk} C_{ij} - \lambda_{fk}.$$

But note that the covariance of security i with any portfolio p will equal a weighted average of the covariances of the security with the securities in the portfolio, using relative portfolio holdings as weights. Here:

$$C_{ik} = \sum_j X_{jk} C_{ij}.$$

Substituting this relationship in the prior equation and rearranging terms gives equation (2).

has invested. To do so requires only a few straightforward operations. In effect, a wealth-weighted average is taken of the first-order conditions for each security. Not surprisingly, the result is similar to that obtained earlier:

$$E_i - \frac{2}{\tau_m} C_{im} = \lambda_{fm} \quad \text{for all i.} \tag{3}$$

Here, τ_m is the wealth-weighted risk tolerance of the investors in the market, or the *societal risk tolerance*. The value of C_{im} represents the covariance of security i with the *market portfolio*, which includes all securities in the market, with each represented in proportion to its outstanding value. The last term is a weighted average of the values of λ_{fk} for the K investors, with the weights depending on the investors' influences in the marketplace, where influence depends on both invested wealth and risk tolerance. It can be interpreted as the *societal marginal utility of wealth.* [11]

---

[11] To derive equation (3) begin by multiplying all terms in equation (2) by τ_k and rearranging slightly, giving:

$$\tau_k E_i - 2C_{ik} = \tau_k \lambda_{fk}.$$

Next, multiply all terms by W_k, then sum over all investors, giving:

$$\sum_k W_k \tau_k E_i - 2 \sum_k W_k C_{ik} = \sum_k W_k \tau_k \lambda_{fk}.$$

Define τ_m as:

$$\tau_m \equiv \sum_k W_k \tau_k.$$

Now consider the second term. Note that:

$$C_{ik} = Cov(\bar{R}_i, \bar{R}_k)$$

where $\bar{R}_i$ and $\bar{R}_k$ are, respectively, the returns on security i and investor k's portfolio. By the properties of covariance:

$$\sum_k W_k C_{ik} = Cov\left(\bar{R}_i, \sum_k W_k \bar{R}_k\right).$$

But the summation on the right-hand side is simply a wealth-weighted average of the returns on the investors' portfolios or, more simply put, the return on the *market portfolio*. Hence the summation on the left-hand side is the covariance of the return on security i with that of the market portfolio, which can be denoted C_{im}. Making these substitutions and dividing all terms by τ_m gives:

$$E_i - \frac{2}{\tau_m} C_{im} = \frac{\sum_k W_k \tau_k \lambda_{fk}}{\tau_m}.$$

The last term is a weighted average of the values of λ_{fk} for the K investors, with the weights given by the product of W_k and τ_k. Denoting this λ_{fm} gives equation (3).

Expected Returns

One of the key implications of the CAPM concerns the relationships among the expected returns of capital assets. It can be obtained by a minor rearrangement of the previous equation to give:

$$E_i = \lambda_{fm} + \frac{2}{\tau_m} C_{im} \quad \text{for all i.} \tag{4}$$

This shows that in equilibrium there is a linear relationship between the expected returns on securities and their covariances with the market portfolio. Usually the relationship is expressed in terms of a security's *beta*, a scaled measure obtained by dividing a security's covariance with the market portfolio by the variance of the market portfolio (V_m). Substituting this measure gives:

$$E_i = \lambda_{fm} + \frac{2V_m}{\tau_m} \beta_{im} \quad \text{for all i.} \tag{5}$$

where:

$$\beta_{im} \equiv \frac{C_{im}}{V_m}$$

Of course, equation (5) is also linear. Moreover, since portfolio expected returns and covariances with the market portfolio are simply value-weighted averages of the corresponding measures for the component securities, it follows that this relationship holds for all portfolios as well as for all securities.

The Risk Premium

Since the previous equation holds for any portfolio, it will hold for the market portfolio itself. Moreover, the beta value of the market portfolio with itself must equal 1. Letting E_m represent the expected return on the market portfolio, these relationships imply that:

$$\frac{E_m - \lambda_{fm}}{V_m} = \frac{2}{\tau_m}. \tag{6}$$

The term on the left-hand side is the *risk premium per unit of variance*. As the equation shows, it is inversely related to societal risk tolerance.

The Security Market Line

Substituting the risk premium per unit of variance for $2/\tau_m$ in the equation for security expected returns gives a more traditional form of the relationship:

$$E_i = \lambda_{fm} + (E_m - \lambda_{fm})\beta_{im} \quad \text{for all i.} \tag{7}$$

A graphical portrayal is termed the *security market line*. The CAPM implies that all securities and portfolios will plot along such a line. Many would argue that this relationship is the most important single conclusion derived from the CAPM. It shows that expected returns will be linearly related to *market risk*, but not, as often believed, to *total risk*.

Riskless Borrowing and Lending

As can be seen from equation (7), λ_{fm} may be interpreted as the expected return on any "zero-beta" portfolio, including the zero-beta portfolio with minimum variance, as suggested by Black (1972). If a riskless asset is available, λ_{fm} will equal R_f, the riskless rate of return. Under these conditions, the Security Market Line relationship can be written:

$$E_i = R_f + (E_m - R_f)\beta_{im} \quad \text{for all i.} \tag{8}$$

Henceforth, we assume that a riskless asset does exist and can be held in positive or negative amounts—i.e. that investors may either lend or borrow at the riskless rate R_f.

The Characteristic Line

The value of β_{im} may be given an interpretation similar to that found in regression analysis utilizing historic data, although in the context of the CAPM it is to be interpreted strictly as an *ex ante* value based on probabilistic beliefs about future outcomes. The relationship between $\tilde{R}_i$ and $\tilde{R}_m$, the stochastic returns on security i and the market portfolio, respectively, can be written as:

$$\tilde{R}_i = a_i + \beta_{im}\tilde{R}_m + \tilde{\varepsilon}_i. \tag{9}$$

Given the manner in which β_{im} is defined, it must be the case that $\tilde{\varepsilon}_i$ is uncorrelated with[12] $\tilde{R}_m$. Moreover, a_i can be defined so that the expected value of $\tilde{\varepsilon}_i$ is zero. However, there is no reason to expect that $\tilde{\varepsilon}_i$—the *residual*

---

[12]but not necessarily independent of

return or *non-market component of return* for security i—will be uncorrelated with the comparable component for security j. [13]

While the CAPM places no restrictions on the correlations of the residual terms, it does restrict the values of the intercept (a_i) terms. Since the expected value of ε_i is zero, the security market line relationship requires that each intercept be related directly to the security's beta value. [14] The CAPM thus implies that:

$$\bar{R}_i = (1 - \beta_{im})R_f + \beta_{im}\bar{R}_m + \tilde{\varepsilon}_i. \tag{10}$$

A graphical portrayal of this relationship is termed a security or portfolio's *characteristic line.*

Factor Models of Security Returns

Much confusion has arisen concerning the relationship between the equilibrium results of the CAPM and the underlying relationships among security returns. As can be seen, the CAPM makes *no* assumptions about the "return generating process." Hence, its results are completely consistent with *any* such process.

Early approaches to portfolio selection[15] assumed that returns were generated by a model similar (but not identical) to that of equation (9), with the further condition that the residual values were uncorrelated across securities. [16] My initial approach to capital asset pricing in Sharpe (1961) made a similar assumption. Such a "single index" or "single factor" model represents a special case of a *factor model of security returns*. Multi-factor models have been explored by a number of researchers and currently enjoy widespread use in financial practice.

---

[13] In fact, this cannot strictly be the case except in economies with infinitely many securities. Since the market-value weighted sum of the left-hand sides of equation (9) equals $\bar{R}_m$, the market-weighted sum of the $\tilde{\varepsilon}_i$ values must be zero. Thus at least two of the $\tilde{\varepsilon}_i$ values must be negatively correlated.

[14] Taking expectations of equation (9) gives:

$$E_i = a_i + \beta_{im}E_m.$$

Comparison with (8) implies that:

$$a_i = (1 - \beta_{im})R_f.$$

[15] such as that suggested by Markowitz (1959) that I further developed in Sharpe (1961, 1963 and 1970).

[16] In such a model the "common factor" can be highly correlated with the return on the market portfolio, but not precisely equal to it if the assumption that the residual values are to be uncorrelated with one another is to be maintained.

A factor model of security returns identifies a relatively few key factors to which a security's return is assumed to be linearly related, in the following manner:

$$\tilde{R}_i = a_i + \sum_l b_{il}\tilde{F}_l + \tilde{\varepsilon}_i. \qquad (11)$$

In such a model the $\tilde{\varepsilon}_i$ values are assumed to be uncorrelated across securities. Ross' (1976) Arbitrage Pricing Theory (APT) concludes that if returns are generated by such a model, expected returns must be approximately linearly related to the b_{il} values if opportunities to gain through arbitrage are to be precluded. However, the APT provides no implications concerning either the signs or the magnitudes of the coefficients in the associated pricing relationship.

It is entirely possible to augment the assumptions of the APT with those of the CAPM (most importantly, the assumption that investors maximize mean-variance utility functions). The resulting implications will then be consistent with both theories. Moreover, by making assumptions about investors' objectives one can obtain precise statements about the signs and magnitudes of the coefficients of the APT pricing relationship, as I have shown in Sharpe (1984).

The Efficiency of the Market Portfolio

A key concept due to Markowitz (1952) is that of the *efficiency* of a portfolio. In the present context a portfolio can be said to be *efficient* if it would be optimal for an investor with some (non-negative) risk tolerance. Comparison of equations (2) and (3) directly implies that the market portfolio is efficient in this sense.

Consider an investor who has a risk tolerance equal to τ_m and holds the market portfolio. Equation (3) shows that the first-order conditions for the maximization of his or her utility will be met for every security. Since the market portfolio will be optimal for such an investor, it must be efficient. More specifically, the market portfolio will be optimal for an investor with the average (societal) risk tolerance.

The Two-fund Separation Theorem

Under the conditions assumed in the CAPM, every investor's optimal portfolio can be obtained by a suitably chosen combination of any two arbitrarily selected efficient portfolios.[17] Two natural choices are those that would be optimal for investors with risk tolerances of zero and τ_m. The former is the minimum-variance portfolio. The latter is, of course, the market portfolio. Following Tobin (1969), this is generally termed the two-fund separation theorem.

When a riskless asset is available, the minimum-variance portfolio will be composed solely of that asset. Thus all investors will hold combinations of the riskless asset and the market portfolio. For investors with risk tolerance greater than τ_m, optimal investment will involve a negative position in the riskless asset and a positive position in the market portfolio—and hence all risky assets. Note, however, that the market portfolio will include the net positive supply of riskless assets in the economy; hence only investors with τ_k values considerably greater than τ_m will actually have to borrow money. Every other investor will select some combination of the riskless asset and the market portfolio, and thus require only non-negative holdings.

Key Implications

The key implications of the CAPM are that:

1. the market portfolio will be efficient,

---

[17]To provide two-fund separation in this case, rewrite equation (2) as follows:

$$\sum_j 2C_{ij} X_{jk} + \tau_k \lambda_{fk} = \tau_k E_i.$$

Portfolio optimality requires that this relationship be satisfied for each of the N securities and that the full-investment constraint be met. This gives rise to a set of N + 1 simultaneous equations that can be written as:

$$\begin{pmatrix} 2C_{11} & \cdots & \cdots & 2C_{1N} & 1 \\ \cdot & & & \cdot & \cdot \\ \cdot & & & \cdot & \cdot \\ 2C_{N1} & \cdots & \cdots & 2C_{NN} & 1 \\ 1 & \cdots & \cdots & 1 & 0 \end{pmatrix} \begin{pmatrix} X_{1k} \\ \cdot \\ \cdot \\ X_{NK} \\ \lambda^*_{fk} \end{pmatrix} = \begin{pmatrix} 0 \\ \cdot \\ \cdot \\ 0 \\ 1 \end{pmatrix} + \begin{pmatrix} E_1 \\ \cdot \\ \cdot \\ E_N \\ 0 \end{pmatrix} \tau_k$$

where λ^*_{fk} represents $\tau_k \lambda_{fk}$. Writing this in matrix notation gives:

$$DY = K + \tau_k F$$

The solution, obtained by multiplying both sides by the inverse of D, is thus:

$$Y = \{D^{-1}K\} + \tau_k\{D^{-1}F\}.$$

Note that the optimal portfolio is a linear function of τ_k. Thus it can be restated as a linear function of any two vectors satisfying the above equation associated with different values of τ_k.

2. all efficient portfolios will be equivalent to investment in the market portfolio plus, possibly, lending or borrowing, and

3. there will be a linear relationship between expected return and beta.

Practical applications of these relationships are many. Investors can easily identify efficient portfolio strategies and such strategies can be effectively implemented through mutual funds and other institutional vehicles. Corporate and governmental decision-makers can use the Security Market Line relationship to determine the desirability of an investment project by comparing its expected return with that available in the capital market for projects with similar beta values (i.e. with similar market risk or sensitivity to economic conditions).

In the frictionless world of the CAPM, each investor chooses a portfolio that maximizes his or her utility. This leads to an efficient distribution of risk in the economy, given, of course, the distribution of wealth among investors.

Negative Holdings

The CAPM assumes that investors can take negative positions in assets. For the riskless asset, the traditional manner in which such a position is achieved involves borrowing money. For a risky asset, the traditional method requires a *short sale*.

A "short position" is achieved by borrowing an asset such as a share of stock, with a promise to repay in kind, typically on demand. The borrowed asset is then sold, generating a cash receipt. If the proceeds of the sale may be used for other types of investment, the overall effect is equivalent to that of a negative holding of the asset in question. If, however, the proceeds are "impounded" to serve as collateral for the borrowed asset, such a short position may differ from a negative holding of the asset in question. In many countries, proceeds from some short sales are impounded in this manner, and the short seller receives little or no interest on the impounded amount. [18] Moreover, some institutional investors are precluded from the use of short positions, either through explicit rules or implicit threat of suit for violation of fiduciary standards. Other restrictions may apply—for example, exchanges may not allow a short sale following a previous decline in the price of the security in question.

Of necessity, arbitrage-based theories allow short positions. Whether

---

[18] Often additional collateral must be "posted" as "margin," but the short seller is generally allowed to receive the earnings associated with the investment of this amount.

such positions will be taken in equilibrium is usually unclear, since the models lack sufficient assumptions (i.e. those concerning utility functions) to characterize equilibrium holdings. More importantly, by the very nature of the arbitrage approach, multiple solutions in terms of holdings are possible in equilibrium due to the presence (or potential presence) of redundant securities.

While the CAPM assumes that investors can take negative positions in any asset, it implies that in equilibrium the only such positions taken will involve the minimum-variance portfolio. When a riskless asset is available, the only negative holdings in equilibrium will involve borrowing by investors with above-average risk tolerance who wish to finance added investment in a portfolio representing the overall capital market.

With costless monitoring of investors' positions, zero transactions costs, and equal information about securities available to all investors, the only restrictions on negative holdings would be those required to achieve payment of the requisite cash flows. An investor's overall portfolio must be such that in each state of the world the sum of the positive cash flows is at least as large as the sum of the negative cash flows required to match the payments made by the issuers of the securities held in negative amounts. If this condition is violated, such securities have not been fully replicated and the investor cannot expect to receive the full price when taking the associated negative positions.

Since all information is not fully public, and monitoring and transactions are costly, institutional arrangements for short selling have traditionally required the posting of separate collateral for each position, with little if any consideration given to the effects of diversification at the portfolio level. Under such conditions it is difficult or expensive for a high risk-tolerance investor to borrow money to finance added investment in a market-like portfolio. Stock index futures contracts now provide investors with a more efficient means for doing so. Before considering them, however, we investigate the characteristics of an extreme case in which no negative positions are allowed.

Capital Asset Prices without Negative Holdings

Assumptions

To explore the effects of constraints on asset holdings we retain all the assumptions of the CAPM and add N*K non-negativity constraints of the form:

$$X_{ik} \geq 0 \quad \text{for all i and k.}$$

Portfolio Optimality

Investor k seeks to maximize U_k subject to a full investment constraint and the relevant non-negativity constraints. This is a *quadratic programming problem.* An exact solution to a portfolio optimization problem of this form can be obtained using the *critical line algorithm* developed by Markowitz (1956).

When the solution is obtained, some values of X_{ik} will be positive. The corresponding securities are said to be *in* the optimal portfolio. The remainder will be at their lower bounds of zero and are said to be *out* of the portfolio.

Each of the securities *in* the optimal portfolio must have the same marginal utility. If this were not the case, it would be possible to reallocate funds from one such security with a lower marginal utility to one with a higher marginal utility, thereby increasing utility without violating either the full investment constraint or any of the non-negativity constraints. The common value of marginal utility for such securities will be the investor's marginal utility of wealth, which we will again denote λ_{fk}.

Each of the securities *out* of the portfolio must have a marginal utility less than (or equal to) that of the securities in the portfolio. If this were not the case, it would be possible to reallocate funds from a security in the portfolio to one out of the portfolio, thereby increasing utility without violating any of the constraints.

These relationships, which derive from more general ones termed *Kuhn-Tucker conditions,* can be written conveniently as:

$$E_i - \frac{2}{\tau_k} C_{ik} = \lambda_{fk} - z_{ik} \quad \text{for all i} \tag{12}$$

where z_{ik} will be zero for securities *in* the portfolio and greater than or equal to zero for securities *out* of the portfolio.

Aggregation

As with the CAPM, we take a wealth-weighted average of the conditions for the optimality of individual investors' portfolios. The result has a similar form:

$$E_i - \frac{2}{\tau_m} C_{im} = \lambda_{fm} - z_{im} \quad \text{for all i.} \tag{13}$$

Not surprisingly, z_{im} is a weighted average of the z_{ik} values for the K investors, with the weights depending on the investors' influences in the marketplace, where influence depends on both wealth and risk tolerance. [19]

Expected Returns

The previous equation can be transformed simply to obtain:

$$E_i = \lambda_{fm} + \frac{2V_m}{\tau_m}\beta_{im} - z_{im} \quad \text{for all i.} \tag{14}$$

Were it not for the last term, there would be a linear relationship between expected return and beta, as in the CAPM. But the last term implies that only securities that are in *every* investor's optimal portfolio will plot along such a line. [20] Every security that is *out* of at least one investor's optimal portfolio will plot below the line. [21] Moreover, the larger the number of investors for whom the lower bound for a security is binding, the larger is the corresponding value of z_{im} likely to be.

It is important to note that the magnitudes of the z_{im} values will be affected by the distribution of risk tolerances across investors. In the special case in which all investors have the same risk tolerance, everyone will choose to hold the market portfolio and all the z_{im} values will equal zero, giving results identical to those of the original CAPM. Loosely speaking, the greater the variation in risk tolerances across investors, the more likely it is that some of the z_{im} values will be positive. Note, however, that in this connection each investor's influence will depend on both his or her wealth and risk tolerance. Unless there is substantial variation in the risk tolerances of the wealthiest investors, the z_{im} values may be very close to zero, giving results very similar to those of the original CAPM.

---

[19] That is,

$$z_{im} \equiv \frac{\sum_k W_k \tau_k}{\tau_m} z_{ik}.$$

[20] Only for such securities will all the z_{ik} values be zero, giving a value of zero for z_{im} (their weighted average).

[21] At least one z_{ik} value will be positive; since the remainder will all equal zero, the value of z_{im} (their weighted average) will be positive.

The Risk Premium

To determine the risk premium in this case, one must take a market value-weighted average of the equilibrium relationships in the previous equation. Doing so gives:

$$\frac{E_m - \lambda_{fm}}{V_m} = \frac{2}{\tau_m} - \frac{z_{mm}}{V_m},$$

(15)

where z_{mm} represents the market value weighted average of the z_{im} values. [22]

Clearly, the risk premium per unit of variance will be a function of the extent to which investors' portfolios are affected by the non-negativity constraints[23].

The Security Market Line Relationship

Given the final term in the previous equation, it is not particularly instructive to derive a counterpart to the security market line of the CAPM. However, equation (14) can stand as the analogue to a security market line for this case. As indicated earlier, the first two terms do indeed provide such a line. However, in this case the line serves as an upper boundary. Some or all of the securities may plot below the line, with the distances dependent on the degree to which the associated non-negativity constraints are binding. Thus there may not be a precise linear relationship between expected returns and beta values.

Riskless Securities

In this case no riskless borrowing is allowed, since negative positions are precluded. The net positive supply of riskless securities will, however, be included in the market portfolio. For any investor for whom the constraint on borrowing is binding, λ_{fk} will exceed R_f. For all others, the two values will be equal. Hence, λ_{fm} will equal or exceed R_f.

---

[22]Multiplying equation (13) by X_{im} and summing over i gives:

$$E_m = \lambda_{fm} + \frac{2V_m}{\tau_m}\beta_{mm} - \sum_i X_{im} z_{im}.$$

Rearranging terms gives equation (15).

[23]moreover, the magnitude of λ_{fm} will also be affected by such restrictions.

The Efficiency of the Market Portfolio

In the CAPM, the marginal utilities of all securities with respect to the holdings in the market portfolio are equal when evaluated using the societal risk tolerance. This is sufficient for the efficiency of the market portfolio. It is also necessary if the market portfolio is to be efficient for an investor with the societal risk tolerance.

More generally, for the market portfolio to be efficient, the marginal utilities of all securities measured relative to the market portfolio must be equal when evaluated using *some* positive risk tolerance. This follows from the fact that the market portfolio includes positive amounts of every security, hence all securities will be *in* such a portfolio.

For this condition to be met, there must be a linear relationship between security expected returns and their beta values. [24] With restrictions on negative holdings this may not be the case, due to the influences of the z_{im} values. [25] Hence the market portfolio may be inefficient. Of course, the extent of the inefficiency will depend on the magnitudes of the z_{im} values—if most are small, the degree of inefficiency of the market portfolio may be inconsequential.

Fund Separation

Markowitz (1959) showed that non-negativity constraints cause the efficient frontier to be piecewise linear in the space of holdings. Within each linear range, efficient portfolios can be obtained by combining any two other portfolios within

---

[24] For all securities in the market portfolio to have the same marginal utilities requires that:

$$E_i - \frac{2}{\tau} C_{im} = \lambda,$$

where τ and λ are positive constants.

Rearranging terms and converting C_{im} to the equivalent value expressed in terms of β_{im} gives:

$$E_i = \lambda + \frac{2V_m}{\tau} \beta_{im}.$$

To meet the condition for efficiency of the market portfolio, there must thus be a strictly linear relationship between E_i and β_{im}. Moreover, the intercept and slope must both be positive, otherwise the implied values of λ and τ, respectively, will be negative.

[25] If all the z_{im} values are zero, of course, the linear relationship will obtain. In the highly unlikely event that there is a linear relationship between the z_{im} values and the corresponding beta values, there will also be a linear relationship between the E_i and β_{im} values.

the range[26]. However, no two portfolios can, in general, be utilized to obtain *all* efficient portfolios. Hence two-fund separation may not strictly apply in this case.

Key Implications

When negative positions are precluded:

1. the market portfolio may not be efficient,
2. some efficient portfolios may not be equivalent to investment in the market portfolio plus, possibly, lending or borrowing, and
3. there may not be a linear relationship between expected return and beta.

All these implications suggest a diminution in the efficiency with which risk can be allocated in an economy. The choice of optimal portfolios becomes more difficult than in the simple setting of the CAPM. Calculations of cost of capital for corporate and governmental investment projects may require more than the determination of a simple relationship between expected return and market risk. More fundamentally, overall welfare may be lower than it would be if the constraints on negative holdings could be reduced or removed.

While the magnitudes of the departures from the implications of the original CAPM might be small even under the extreme conditions assumed in this case, it is clear that institutional arrangements to improve investors' abilities to take negative positions can increase the efficiency with which risk is allocated in an economy. Following some comments on financial innovation in general, I will discuss the stock index futures contract—an innovation that provides such an improvement.

Financial Innovation

More than most sciences, economics not only analyzes reality, it also alters it. Theory leads to empiricism which changes behavior. Nowhere is this more evident than in financial economics. The academic field of finance differs radically from that of three decades ago, due in large part to advances in financial economic theory and to the extensive empirical research that has flowed from those advances. At least as important, the practice of finance has been affected in fundamental ways by the progress in financial economics. Most notably, the

---

[26]those lying at the end-points provide convenient choices

last decade has been marked by unprecedented innovation in financial instruments, markets and institutions.

Given the bewildering pace of such innovation, it is not surprising that some individuals and organizations have at times found it difficult to fully understand the proper uses of some of the new instruments and procedures. Evidence abounds that those who fail to learn the principles of financial economics in more formal ways will do so through experience. Markets are effective although sometimes cruel teachers. In general, financial systems are self-correcting. Given time, participants learn to use new instruments and procedures to improve overall welfare, not just to reallocate wealth from one set of hands to another. It is usually best to wait until the forces of competition are able to regulate a market rather than to impose regulations prematurely.

Much financial innovation has been possible due to the remarkable advances in computation and communication technology. Moreover, increased global competition, with the accompanying diminution of monopoly power on the part of organizations and governments, has played an important role. Nonetheless, I cannot help but believe that discoveries in the science of financial economics have had a major influence. Stock index futures contracts appear to provide a clear example of this.

Stock Index Futures Contracts

Features

A traditional *forward contract* is an agreement on the part of the seller to deliver a stated amount of a commodity on a given future date to the buyer at a pre-specified price. A *futures contract* is a standardized forward contract with the further provision that the delivery price be reset at the end of each trading day to equal the price at which new agreements were struck. At the time of each such resetting, one of the two parties pays the other an amount equal to the difference between the new price and the old. This process is known as "posting variation margin" as a result of the "marking to market" of the price of the contract.

The seller of a futures contract is said to be *short* the contract; the buyer is said to be *long*.

Futures exchanges make it possible for the two parties in a contract to be "unlinked." Thus *A* may sell a contract to *B*. *B* may later sell it to *C* without *A*'s involvement. And later, C may sell it to A, extinguishing it before the final delivery date.

To protect the other party in such an arrangement, each party must post collateral as "margin." The amount need only cover potential losses between two trading days, however, due to the process of marking to market. Margins equal to 10% to 20% of the value of a position typically suffice. To insure that collateral is maintained, yet preserve the standardization of the contract, brokers representing those with positions utilize a *clearing house*, which provides assurance that obligations will be met.

A *financial futures contract* may call for the actual delivery of a stated financial instrument or one or more of a set of such instruments. Alternatively, it may call only for a final marking to market on the delivery day, with one party paying the other an amount equal to the difference between the prior futures price and the value of the underlying financial instrument on the delivery day. The latter is often termed *cash delivery*.

A *stock index futures contract* covers a pre-specified portfolio of stocks. It allows investors to take long or short positions in diversified portfolios. Most such contracts provide for *cash delivery*.

Effects

A key aspect of a stock index futures contract is its focus on a *diversified portfolio* rather than on an individual security or commodity. In this respect, such a contract is similar to a mutual fund, unit trust, commingled index fund or stock index option. All provide investors with "packages" of securities, substantially reducing the costs associated with diversification. Recent growth in investors' reliance on all such vehicles stands, at least in part, as testimony to the influence of financial economics on the process by which risk is borne in modern economies.

A second feature of a stock index futures contract is of particular interest in the present context. Such a contract provides an efficient method for simultaneously taking a positive position in a diversified stock portfolio and a negative position in a riskless asset. In effect, the purchaser of such a contract borrows money to purchase a stock portfolio while the seller lends money and takes a short position in the stock portfolio. [27] If the buyer of the contract posts as margin riskless securities with a value equal to that of the futures position,

---

[27]For details see, for example, Duffie (1989).

the net effect is similar to that of investing a comparable amount in the stocks in the associated index. If less than 100% margin is posted, the effect is similar to that of a levered purchase of the stocks in the index. While not precisely the same as borrowing at the riskless rate to purchase a portfolio of stocks, a long position in a futures contract can provide a very close approximation to such a strategy. Moreover, the upper limit on the borrowing implicit in the arrangement is sufficiently large to satisfy all but a potentially few investors with extremely high risk tolerances.

It is striking that a levered holding of a highly diversified portfolio (i.e. the market portfolio) is precisely the optimal investment strategy for high risk tolerance investors in the simple setting of the original CAPM. While no financial futures contract corresponds to the overall market portfolio, combinations of existing contracts (including those on bonds and other types of securities) may approximate such a strategy.

In a sense, the seller of a futures contract holds negative positions in the underlying securities, and the existence of such positions is inconsistent with the implications of the CAPM. However, when viewed more broadly, this inconsistency may be more apparent than real. Often the seller of a stock index futures contract also holds the individual securities that make up the index in question. The futures position thus provides a *hedge* against changes in the value of the portfolio of actual stocks. As a result, the hedged futures seller's *net* position is virtually risk-free and hence equivalent to investment in a riskless asset. Such a person can assemble the securities in an economical manner and, in effect, provide a means for others to buy or sell the package without incurring the costs associated with the purchase or sale of large numbers of individual stocks. In effect, he or she loans money to the high risk-tolerance investor to enable the latter to purchase added amounts of risky securities.

Futures contracts written on diversified portfolios require less margin than would a set of contracts of individual securities, each with its own required margin. Moreover, stock index contracts take advantage of economies of scale in transactions and recordkeeping.

In effect, stock index futures contracts provide those who might be limited by traditional constraints on borrowing with a means for achieving desirable investment strategies. Moreover, the strategies are similar to those that are optimal for high risk-tolerance investors in the setting of the original CAPM. Hence, the existence of such contracts may well bring actual capital markets closer to those of this simple equilibrium theory. If so, stock index futures contracts may significantly improve the efficiency with which risk is allocated in an economy.

Conclusions

Here I have explicitly considered only one type of impediment to the efficient allocation of risk. However, this case can serve as a representative of many others. The greater the costs and constraints associated with the purchase and sale of securities, the farther will an economy be from the goal of allocating risk to those most able and willing to bear it.

Happily, technological advances and greater understanding of the principles of financial economics are reducing costs and constraints of this type at a rapid pace. As a result, capital markets are moving closer to the conditions assumed in some of the simpler types of financial theory. Far more important: the combined efforts of theoreticians, empiricists and practitioners are increasing the efficiency with which risk is allocated among individuals, leading to improvements in social welfare.

References

Arrow, K. (1953), "Le Role des Valeurs Boursieres pour la repartition la Meilleure des Risques," *Econometrie*, Colloques Internationaux du Centre National de la Recherche Scientifique, Vol. XI, Paris, 41–47.

Black, F. (1972), "Capital Market Equilibrium with Restricted Borrowing," *Journal of Business*, 45:444–454.

Black, F. and M. Scholes (1973), "The Pricing of Options and Corporate Liabilities," *Journal of Political Economy*, 81:637–654.

Breeden, D. (1979), "An Intertemporal Asset Pricing Model with Stochastic Consumption and Investment Opportunities," *Journal of Financial Economics*, 7:265–296.

Brennan, M. J. (1970), "Taxes, Market Valuation and Corporate Financial Policy," *National Tax Journal*, December 1970, pp. 417–427.

Cox, J., S. Ross and M. Rubinstein (1979), "Option Pricing: A Simplified Approach," *Journal of Financial Economics*, 7, pp. 229–263.

Debreu, G. (1959), *Theory of Value*, New York: John Wiley and Sons.

Duffie, D. (1989), *Futures Markets*, Englewood Cliffs, New Jersey: Prentice Hall.

Glenn, D. (1976), "Super Premium Security Prices and Optimal Corporate Financing Decisions," *Journal of Finance*, May 1976.

Kraus, A. and R. Litzenberger (1976), "Skewness Preference and the Valuation of Risk Assets," *Journal of Finance*, 38:1085–1100.

Levy, H. (1978), "Equilibrium in an Imperfect Market: A Constraint on the Number of Securities in a Portfolio," *American Economic Review*, 68:643–658.

Levy, H. and H. Markowitz (1979), "Approximating Expected Utility by a Function of Mean and Variance," *American Economic Review*, June 1979.

Lintner, J. (1965), "The Valuation of Risk Assets and the Selection of Risky Investments in Stock Portfolios and Capital Budgets," *Review of Economics and Statistics*, 47:13–37.

Lintner, J. (1969), "The Aggregation of Investors' Diverse Judgements and Preferences in Purely Competitive Markets," *Journal of Financial and Quantitative Analysis*, 4:346–382.

Markowitz, H. (1952), "Portfolio Selection," *Journal of Finance*, 7:7791.

Markowitz, H. (1956), "The Optimization of a Quadratic Function Subject to Linear Constraints," *Naval Research Logistics Quarterly*, 3, pp. 111–133.

Markowitz, H. (1959), *Portfolio Selection: Efficient Diversification of Investments*, New York: John Wiley and Sons, Inc.

Markowitz, H. (1987), *Mean-Variance Analysis in Portfolio Choice and Capital Markets*, New York: Basil Blackwell Inc.

Markowitz, H. (1990), "Risk Adjustment," *Journal of Accounting, Auditing and Finance*, forthcoming.

Merton, R. (1973), "An Intertemporal Capital Asset Pricing Model," *Econometrica*, 41:867–887.

Merton, R. (1987), "A Simple Model of Capital Market Equilibrium With Incomplete Information," *Journal of Finance*, 52:483–510.

Modigliani, F. and M. Miller (1958), "The Cost of Capital, Corporation Finance, and the Theory of Investment," *American Economic Review*, 48:261–297.

Mossin, J. (1966), "Equilibrium in a Capital Asset Market," *Econometrica*, 35: pp. 768–783.

Ross, S. (1976), "Arbitrage Theory of Capital Asset Pricing," *Journal of Economic Theory*, 13: pp. 341–360.

Rubinstein, M. (1974), "An Aggregation Theorem for Securities Markets," *Journal of Financial Economics*, 1:225–244.

Sharpe, W. (1961), "Portfolio Analysis Based on a Simplified Model of the Relationships Among Securities," PhD Dissertation, University of California at Los Angeles, June 1961.

Sharpe, W. (1963), "A Simplified Model for Portfolio Analysis," *Management Science*, 9:277–293.

Sharpe, W. (1964), "Capital Asset Prices: A Theory of Market Equilibrium Under Conditions of Risk," *Journal of Finance*, 19:425–442.

Sharpe, W. (1970), *Portfolio Theory and Capital Markets*, New York: McGraw–Hill.

Sharpe, W. (1978), *Investments*, Englewood Cliffs, New Jersey: Prentice–Hall.

Sharpe, W. (1984), "Factor Models, CAPMs, and the APT," *Journal of Portfolio Management*, Fall 1984, pp. 21–25.

Tobin, J. (1969), "Liquidity Preference as Behavior Towards Risk," *Review of Economic Studies*, 25:65–86.

Von Neumann, J. and O. Morgenstern (1944), *Theory of Games and Economic Behavior*, Princeton: Princeton University Press.

A Simplified Model for Portfolio Analysis*

William F. Sharpe†

This paper describes the advantages of using a particular model of the relationships among securities for practical applications of the Markowitz portfolio analysis technique. A computer program has been developed to take full advantage of the model: 2,000 securities can be analyzed at an extremely low cost—as little as 2% of that associated with standard quadratic programming codes. Moreover, preliminary evidence suggests that the relatively few parameters used by the model can lead to very nearly the same results obtained with much larger sets of relationship among securities. The possibility of low-cost analysis, coupled with a likelihood that a relatively small amount of information need be sacrificed make the model an attractive candidate for initial practical applications of the Markowitz technique.

*Received December 1961.

†The author wishes to express his appreciation for the cooperation of the staffs of both the Western Data Processing Center at UCLA and the Pacific Northwest Research Computer Laboratory at the University of Washington where the program was tested. His greatest debt, however, is to Dr. Harry M. Markowitz of the RAND Corporation, with whom he was privileged to have a number of stimulating conversations during the past year. It is no longer possible to segregate the ideas in this paper into those which were his, those which were the author's, and those which were developed jointly. Suffice it to say that the only accomplishments which are unquestionably the property of the author are those of authorship—first of the computer program and then of this article.

Reprinted from *Management Science* 7 (January 1963), pp. 277–293, by permission of the author and the publisher.

1.   Introduction

Markowitz has suggested that the process of portfolio selection be approached by (1) making probabilistic estimates of the future performances of securities, (2) analyzing those estimates to determine an *efficient set* of portfolios and (3) selecting from that set the portfolios best suited to the investor's preferences [1, 2, 3]. This paper extends Markowitz' work on the second of these three stages—*portfolio analysis*. The preliminary sections state the problem in its general form and describe Markowitz' solution technique. The remainder of the paper presents a simplified model of the relationships among securities, indicates the manner in which it allows the portfolio analysis problem to be simplified, and provides evidence on the costs as well as the desirability of using the model for practical applications of the Markowitz technique.

2.   The Portfolio Analysis Problem

A security analyst has provided the following predictions concerning the future returns from each of N securities:

$E_i \equiv$ the expected value of R_i (the return from security i)
C_{i1} through C_{in}; C_{ij} represents the covariance between R_i and R_j (as usual, when $i = j$ the figure is the variance of R_i)

The portfolio analysis problem is as follows. Given such a set of predictions, determine the set of *efficient portfolios*; a portfolio is efficient if none other gives either (a) a higher expected return and the same variance of return or (b) a lower variance of return and the same expected return.

Let X_i represent the proportion of a portfolio invested in security i. Then the expected return (E) and variance of return (V) of any portfolio can be expressed in terms of (a) the basic data (E_i-*values and* C_{ij}-*values*) and (b) the amounts invested in various securities:

$$E = \sum_i X_i E_i$$

$$V = \sum_i \sum_j X_i X_j C_{ij}.$$

Consider an objective function of the form:

$$\phi = \lambda E - V$$

$$= \lambda \sum_i X_i E_i - \sum_i \sum_j X_i X_j C_{ij}.$$

Given a set of values for the parameters (λ, E_i's and C_{ij}'s), the value of ϕ can be changed by varying the X_i values as desired, as long as two basic restrictions are observed:

1. The entire portfolio must be invested:[1]

$$\sum_i X_i = 1$$

and 2. no security may be held in negative quantities:[2]

$$X_i \geqq 0 \quad \text{for all } i.$$

A portfolio is described by the proportions invested in various securities—in our notation by the values of X_i. For each set of admissable [*sic*] values of the X_i variables there is a corresponding predicted combination of E and V and thus of ϕ. Figure 1 illustrates this relationship for a particular value of λ. The line ϕ_1 shows the combinations of E and V which give $\phi = \phi_1$, where $\phi = \lambda_k E - V$; the other lines refer to larger values of $\phi (\phi_3 > \phi_2 > \phi_1)$. Of all possible portfolios, one will maximize the value of ϕ;[3] in figure 1 it is portfolio C. The relationship between this solution and the portfolio analysis problem is obvious. The E, V combination obtained will be on the boundary of the set of attainable combinations; moreover, the objective function will be tangent to the set at that point. Since this function is of the form

$$\phi = \lambda E - V$$

the slope of the boundary at the point must be λ; thus, by varying λ from $+ \infty$ to 0, every solution of the portfolio analysis problem can be obtained.

For any given value of λ the problem described in this section requires the maximization of a quadratic function, ϕ (which is a function of X_i, X_i^2, and

---

[1]Since cash can be included as one of the securities (explicitly or implicitly) this assumption need cause no lack of realism.

[2]This is the standard formulation. Cases in which short sales are allowed require a different approach.

[3]This fact is crucial to the critical line computing procedure described in the next section.

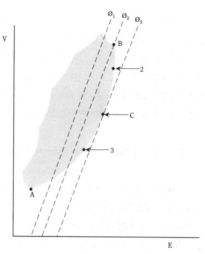

Figure 1

$X_i X_j$ terms) subject to a linear constraint ($\Sigma_i X_i = 1$), with the variables restricted to non-negative values. A number of techniques have been developed to solve such *quadratic programming problems*. The critical line method, developed by Markowitz in conjunction with his work on portfolio analysis, is particularly suited to this problem and was used in the program described in this paper.

3. The Critical Line Method

Two important characteristics of the set of efficient portfolios make systematic solution of the portfolio analysis problem relatively straightforward. The first concerns the relationships among portfolios. Any set of efficient portfolios can be described in terms of a smaller set of *corner portfolios*. Any point of the E, V curve (other than the points associated with corner portfolios) can be obtained with a portfolio constructed by dividing the total investment between the two adjacent corner portfolios. For example, the portfolio which gives E, V combination C in Figure 1 might be some linear combination of the two corner portfolios with E, V combinations shown by points 2 and 3. This characteristic allows the analyst to restrict his attention to corner portfolios rather than the complete set of efficient portfolios; the latter can be readily derived from the former.

The second characteristic of the solution concerns the relationships among corner portfolios. Two corner portfolios which are adjacent on the E, V

curve are related in the following manner: one portfolio will contain either (1) all the securities which appear in the other, plus one additional security or (2) all but one of the securities which appear in the other. Thus in moving down the E, V curve from one corner portfolio to the next, the quantities of the securities in efficient portfolios will vary until either one drops out of the portfolio or another enters. The point at which a change takes place marks a new corner portfolio.

The major steps in the critical line method for solving the portfolio analysis problem are:

1. The corner portfolio with $\lambda = \infty$ is determined. It is composed entirely of the one security with the highest expected return. [4]

2. Relationships between (a) the amounts of the various securities contained in efficient portfolios and (b) the value of λ are computed. It is possible to derive such relationships for any section of the E, V curve between adjacent corner portfolios. The relationships which apply to one section of the curve will not, however, apply to any other section.

3. Using the relationships computed in (2), each security is examined to determine the value of λ at which a change in the securities included in the portfolio would come about:

   a. securities presently in the portfolio are examined to determine the value of λ at which they would drop out, and

   b. securities not presently in the portfolio are examined to determine the value of λ at which they would enter the portfolio.

4. The next largest value of λ at which a security either enters or drops out of the portfolio is determined. This indicates the location of the next corner portfolio.

5. The composition of the new corner portfolio is computed, using the relationships derived in (2). However, since these relationships held only for the section of the curve between this corner portfolio and the preceding one, the solution process can only continue if new relationships are derived. The method thus returns to step (2) unless $\lambda = 0$, in which case the analysis is complete.

---

[4] In the event that two or more of the securities have the same (highest) expected return, the first efficient portfolio is the combination of such securities with the lowest variance.

The amount of computation required to complete a portfolio analysis using this method is related to the following factors:

1. The number of securities analyzed

    This will affect the extent of the computation in step (2) and the number of computations in step (3).

2. The number of corner portfolios

    Steps (2) through (5) must be repeated once to find each corner portfolio.

3. The complexity of the variance-covariance matrix

    Step (2) requires a matrix be inverted and must be repeated once for each corner portfolio.

The amount of computer memory space required to perform a portfolio analysis will depend primarily on the size of the variance-covariance matrix. In the standard case, if N securities are analyzed this matrix will have $\frac{1}{2}(N^2 + N)$ elements.

4.   The Diagonal Model

Portfolio analysis requires a large number of comparisons; obviously the practical application of the technique can be greatly facilitated by a set of assumptions which reduces the computational task involved in such comparisons. One such set of assumptions (to be called the diagonal model) is described in this article. This model has two virtues: it is one of the simplest which can be construed without assuming away the existence of interrelationships among securities and there is considerable evidence that it can capture a large part of such interrelationships.

The major characteristic of the diagonal model is the assumption that the returns of various securities are related only through common relationships with some basic underlying factor. The return from any security is determined solely by random factors and this single outside element; more explicitly:

$$R_i = A_i + B_i I + C_i$$

where A_i and B_i are parameters, C_i is a random variable with an expected value of zero and variance Q_i, and I is the level of some index. The index, I, may be the level of the stock market as a whole, the Gross National Product, some price index or any other factor thought to be the most important single

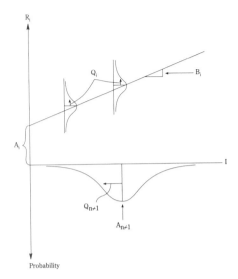

Figure 2

influence on the returns from securities. The future level of I is determined in part by random factors:

$$I = A_{n+1} + C_{n+1}$$

where A_{n+1} is a parameter and C_{n+1} is a random variable with an expected value of zero and a variance of Q_{n+1}. It is assumed that the covariance between C_i and C_j is zero for all values of i and j ($i \neq j$).

Figure 2 provides a graphical representation of the model. A_i and B_i serve to locate the line which relates the expected value of R_i to the level of I. Q_i indicates the variance of R_i around the expected relationship (this variance is assumed to be the same at each point along the line). Finally, A_{n+1} indicates the expected value of I and Q_{n+1} the variance around that expected value.

The diagonal model requires the following predictions from a security analyst:

    1) values of A_i, B_i and Q_i for each of N securities

    2) values of A_{n+1} and Q_{n+1} for the index I.

The number of estimates required from the analyst is thus greatly reduced: from $5,150$ to 302 for an analysis of 100 securities and from $2,003,000$ to $6,002$ for an analysis of $2,000$ securities.

Once the parameters of the diagonal model have been specified all the inputs required for the standard portfolio analysis problem can be derived. The relationships are:

$$E_i = A_i + B_i(A_{n+1})$$

$$V_i = (B_i)^2(Q_{n+1}) + Q_i$$

$$C = (B_i)(B_j)(Q_{n+1})$$

A portfolio analysis could be performed by obtaining the values required by the diagonal model, calculating from them the full set of data required for the standard portfolio analysis problem and then performing the analysis with the derived values. However, additional advantages can be obtained if the portfolio analysis problem is restated directly in terms of the parameters of the diagonal model. The following section describes the manner in which such a restatement can be performed.

5. The Analogue

The return from a portfolio is the weighted average of the returns from its component securities:

$$R_p = \sum_{i=1}^{N} X_i R_i$$

The contribution of each security to the total return of a portfolio is simply $X_i\,R_i$ or, under the assumptions of the diagonal model:

$$X_i(A_i + B_i I + C_i).$$

The total contribution of a security to the return of the portfolio can be broken into two components: (1) an investment in the "basic characteristics" of the security in question and (2) an "investment" in the index.

(1) $\quad X_i(A_i + B_i I + C_i) = X_i(A_i + C_i)$

(2) $\qquad\qquad\qquad + X_i B_i I$

The return of a portfolio can be considered to be the result of (1) a series of investments in N "basic securities" and (2) an investment in the index:

$$R_p = \sum_{i=1}^{N} X_i(A_i + C_i) + \left[\sum_{i=1}^{N} X_i B_i \right] I$$

Defining X_{n+1} as the weighted average responsiveness of R_p to the level of I:

$$X_{n+1} \equiv \sum_{i=1}^{N} X_i B_i$$

and substituting this variable and the formula for the determinants of I, we obtain:

$$R_p = \sum_{i=1}^{N} X_i(A_i + C_i) + X_{n+1}(A_{n+1} + C_{n+1})$$

$$= \sum_{i=1}^{N+1} X_i(A_i + C_i).$$

The expected return of a portfolio is thus:

$$E = \sum_{i=1}^{N+1} X_i A_i$$

while the variance is:[5]

$$V = \sum_{i=1}^{N+1} X_i^2 Q_i$$

This formulation indicates the reason for use of the parameters A_{n+1} and Q_{n+1} to describe the expected value and variance of the future value of I. It also indicates the reason for calling this the "diagonal model". The variance-covariance matrix, which is full when N securities are considered, can be expressed as a matrix with non-zero elements only along the diagonal by including an $(n+1)$st security defined as indicated. This vastly reduces the number of computations required to solve the portfolio analysis problem (primarily in step 2 of the critical line method, when the variance-covariance

---

[5]Recall that the diagonal model assumes cov $(C_i, C_j) = 0$ for all i and j $(i \neq j)$.

matrix must be inverted) and allows the problem to be stated directly in terms of the basic parameters of the diagonal model:

Maximize: $\lambda E - V$

Where: $E = \displaystyle\sum_{i=1}^{N+1} X_i A_i$

$V = \displaystyle\sum_{i=1}^{N+1} X_i^2 Q_i$

Subject to: $X_i \geqq 0$ for all i from 1 to N

$\displaystyle\sum_{i=1}^{N} X_i = 1$

$\displaystyle\sum_{i=1}^{N} X_i B_i = X_{n+1}.$

6.   The Diagonal Model Portfolio Analysis Code

As indicated in the previous section, if the portfolio analysis problem is expressed in terms of the basic parameters of the diagonal model, computing time and memory space required for solution can be greatly reduced. This section describes a machine code, written in the FØRTRAN language, which takes full advantage of the characteristics of the diagonal model. It uses the critical line method to solve the problem stated in the previous section.

The computing time required by the diagonal code is considerably smaller than that required by standard quadratic programming codes. The RAND QP code[6] required 33 minutes to solve a 100-security example on an IBM 7090 computer; the same problem was solved in 30 seconds with the diagonal code. Moreover, the reduced storage requirements allow many more securities to be

---

[6]The program is described in [4]. Several alternative quadratic programming codes are available. A recent code, developed by IBM, which uses the critical line method is likely to prove considerably more efficient for the portfolio analysis problem. The RAND code is used for comparison since it is the only standard program with which the author has had experience.

analyzed: with the IBM 709 or 7090 the RAND QP code can be used for no more than 249 securities, while the diagonal code can analyze up to 2,000 securities.

Although the diagonal code allows the total computing time to be greatly reduced, the cost of a large analysis is still far from insignificant. Thus there is every incentive to limit the computations to those essential for the final selection of a portfolio. By taking into account the possibilities of borrowing and lending money, the diagonal code restricts the computations to those absolutely necessary for determination of the final set of efficient portfolios. The importance of these alternatives, their effect on the portfolio analysis problem and the manner in which they are taken into account in the diagonal code are described in the remainder of this section.

A. The "lending portfolio"

There is some interest rate (r_l) at which money can be lent with virtual assurance that both principal and interest will be returned; at the least, money can be buried in the ground $(r_l = 0)$. Such an alternative could be included as one possible security $(A_i = 1 + r_l, B_i = 0, Q_i = 0)$ but this would necessitate some needless computation. [7] In order to minimize computing time, lending at some pure interest rate is taken into account explicitly in the diagonal code.

The relationship between lending and efficient portfolios can best be seen in terms of an E, σ curve showing the combinations of expected return and standard deviation of return $(= \sqrt{V})$ associated with efficient portfolios. Such a curve is shown in Figure 3 (FBCG); point A indicates the E, σ combination attained if all funds are lent. The relationship between lending money and purchasing portfolios can be illustrated with the portfolio which has the E, σ combination shown by point Z. Consider a portfolio with X_z invested in portfolio Z and the remainder $(1 - X_z)$ lent at the rate r_l. The expected return from such a portfolio would be:

$$E = X_z E_z + (1 - X_z)(1 + r_l)$$

and the variance of return would be:

$$V = X_z^2 V_z + (1 - X_z)^2 V_l + 2 X_z (1 - X_z)(cov_{zl})$$

---

[7] Actually, the diagonal code cannot accept non-positive values of Q_i; thus if the lending alternative is to be included as simply another security, it must be assigned a very small value of Q_i. This procedure will give virtually the correct solution but is inefficient.

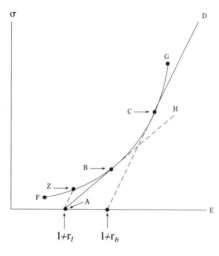

Figure 3

But, since V_l and cov_{zl} are both zero:

$$V = X_z^2 V_z$$

and the standard deviation of return is:

$$\sigma = X_z \sigma_z.$$

Since both E and σ are linear functions of X_z, the E, σ combinations of all portfolios made up of portfolio Z plus lending must lie on a straight line connecting points Z and A. In general, by splitting his investment between a portfolio and lending, an investor can attain any E, σ combination on the line connecting the E, σ combinations of the two components.

Many portfolios which are efficient in the absence of the lending alternative becomes [*sic*] inefficient when it is introduced. In Figure 3, for example, the possibility of attaining E, σ combinations along the line AB makes all portfolios along the original E, σ curve from point F to point B inefficient. For any desired level of E below that associated with portfolio B, the most efficient portfolio will be some combination of portfolio B and lending. Portfolio B can be termed the "lending portfolio" since it is the appropriate portfolio whenever some of the investor's funds are to be lent at the rate r_l. This portfolio can be found readily once the E, σ curve is known. It lies at the point on the curve at which a ray from ($E = 1 + r_l$, $\sigma = 0$) is tangent to the curve. If the E, σ curve is not known in its entirety it is still possible to determine whether or not a particular portfolio is the lending portfolio by computing the rate of interest which *would* make the portfolio in question the lending portfolio. For example, the rate of interest associated in this manner with portfolio C is r_b, found by extending a tangent to the curve down to the E-axis. The diagonal code computes such a rate of interest for each corner portfolio as the analysis proceeds; when it falls below the previously stated lending rate the code computes the composition of the lending portfolio and terminates the analysis.

B. *The "borrowing portfolio"*

In some cases an investor may be able to borrow funds in order to purchase even greater amounts of a portfolio than his own funds will allow. If the appropriate rate for such borrowing were r_b, illustrated in figure 3, the E, σ combinations attainable by purchasing portfolio C with both the investor's funds and with borrowed funds would lie along the line CD, depending on the amount borrowed. Inclusion of the borrowing alternative makes certain portfolios inefficient which are efficient in the absence of the alternative; in this case the affected portfolios are those with E, σ combinations along the segment of the original E, σ curve from C to G. Just as there is a single appropriate portfolio if any lending is contemplated, there is a single appropriate portfolio if borrowing is contemplated. This "borrowing portfolio" is related to the rate of interest at which funds can be borrowed in exactly the same manner as the "lending portfolio" is related to the rate at which funds can be lent.

The diagonal code does not take account of the borrowing alternative in the manner used for the lending alternative since it is necessary to compute all previous corner portfolios in order to derive the portion of the E, σ curve below the borrowing portfolio. For this reason all computations required to derive the full E, σ curve above the lending portfolio must be made. However, the code does allow the user to specify the rate of interest at which funds can be borrowed. If this alternative is chosen, none of the corner portfolios which will be inefficient when borrowing is considered will be printed. Since as much as 65% of the total computer time can be spent recording (on tape) the results of the analysis this is not an insignificant saving.

7.   The Cost of Portfolio Analysis with the Diagonal Code

The total time (and thus cost) required to perform a portfolio analysis with the diagonal code will depend upon the number of securities analyzed, the number of corner portfolios and, to some extent, the composition of the corner portfolios. A formula which gives quite an accurate estimate of the time required to perform an analysis on an IBM 709 computer was obtained by analyzing a series of runs during which the time required to complete each major segment of the program was recorded. The approximate time required for the analysis will be: [8]

Number of seconds = .6

+ .114 × number of securities analyzed

+ .54 × number of corner portfolios

+ .0024 × number of securities analyzed × number of corner portfolios.

Unfortunately only the number of securities analyzed is known before the analysis is begun. In order to estimate the cost of portfolio analysis before it is performed, some relationship between the number of corner portfolios and the number of securities analyzed must be assumed. Since no theoretical relationship can be derived and since the total number of corner portfolios could be several times the number of securities analysed [sic], it seemed desirable to obtain some crude notion of the typical relationship when "reasonable" inputs are used. To accomplish this, a series of portfolio analyses was performed using inputs generated by a Monte Carlo model.

Data were gathered on the annual returns during the period 1940-1951 for 96 industrial common stocks chosen randomly from the New York Stock Exchange. The returns of each security were then related to the level of a stock market index and estimates of the parameters of the diagonal model obtained. These parameters were assumed to be samples from a population of A_i, B_i and Q_i triplets related as follows:

$$A_i = \overline{A} + r_1$$

$$B_i = \overline{B} + \psi A_i + r_2$$

$$Q_i = \overline{Q} + \theta A_i + \gamma B_i + r_3$$

---

[8]The computations in this section are based on the assumption that no corner portfolios prior to the lending portfolio are printed. If the analyst chooses to print all preceding portfolios, the estimates given in this section should be multiplied by 2.9; intermediate cases can be estimated by interpolation.

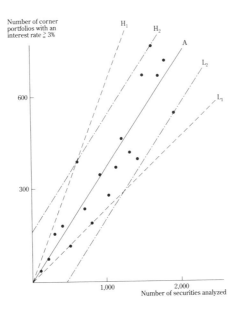

Figure 4

where r_1, r_2 and r_3 are random variables with zero means. Estimates for the parameters of these three equations were obtained by regression analysis and estimates of the variances of the random variables determined.[9] With this information the characteristics of any desired number of securities could be generated. A random number generator was used to select a value for A_i; this value, together with an additional random number determined the value of B_i; the value of Q_i was then determined with a third random number and the previously obtained values of A_i and B_i.

Figure 4 shows the relationship between the number of securities analyzed and the number of corner portfolios with interest rates greater than 3% (an approximation to the "lending rate"). Rather than perform a sophisticated analysis of these data, several lines have been used to bracket the results in various ways. These will be used subsequently as extreme cases, on the presumption that most practical cases will lie within these extremes (but with no presumption that these limits will never be exceeded). Curve *A* indicates the

---

[9]The random variables were considered normally distributed; in one case, to better approximate the data, two variances were used for the distribution—one for the portion above the mean and another for the portion below the mean.

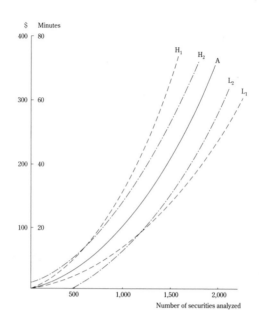

Figure 5

average relationship between the number of portfolios and the number of securities: average $(N_p/N_s) = .37$. Curve H_1 indicates the highest such relationship: maximum $(N_p/N_s) = .63$; the line L_1 indicates the lowest: minimum $(N_p/N_s) = .24$. The other two curves, H_2 and L_2, indicate respectively the maximum deviation above (155) and below (173) the number of corner portfolios indicated by the average relationship $N_p = .37 N_s$.

In Figure 5 the total time required for a portfolio analysis is related to the number of securities analyzed under various assumptions about the relationship between the number of corner portfolios and the number of securities analyzed. Each of the curves shown in Figure 5 is based on the corresponding curve in Figure 4; for example, curve A in Figure 5 indicates the relationship between total time and number of securities analyzed on the assumption that the relationship between the number of corner portfolios and the number of securities is that shown by curve A in Figure 4. For convenience a second scale has been provided in Figure 5, showing the total cost of the analysis on the assumption that an IBM 709 computer can be obtained at a cost of $300 per hour.

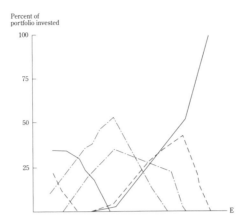

Figure 6A   Composition of Efficient Portfolios Derived from the Analysis of the Parameters of the Diagonal Model.

8.   The Value of Portfolio Analysis Based on the Diagonal Model

The assumptions of the diagonal model lie near the end of the spectrum of possible assumptions about the relationships among securities. The model's extreme simplicity enables the investigator to perform a portfolio analysis at a very small cost, as we have shown. However, it is entirely possible that this simplicity so restricts the security analyst in making his predictions that the value of the resulting portfolio analysis also very small.

In order to estimate the ability of the diagonal model to summarize information concerning the performance of securities a simple test was performed. Twenty securities were chosen randomly from the New York Stock Exchange and their performance during the period 1940–1951 used to obtain two sets of data: (1) the actual mean returns, variances of returns and covariances of returns during the period and (2) the parameters of the diagonal model, estimated by regression techniques from the performance of the securities during the period. A portfolio analysis was then performed on each set of data. The results are summarized in Figures 6a and 6b. Each security which entered any of the efficient portfolios in significant amounts is represented by a particular type of line; the height of each line above any given value of E indicates the percentage of the efficient portfolio with that particular E

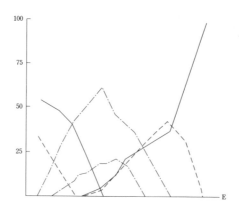

Figure 6B   Compostition of Efficient Portfolios Derived from the Analysis of Historical Data.

composed of the security in question. The two figures thus indicate the compositions of all the efficient portfolios chosen from the analysis of the historical data (Figure 6b) and the compositions of all the portfolios chosen from the analysis of the parameters of the diagonal model (Figure 6a). The similarity of the two figures indicates that the 62 parameters of the diagonal model were able to capture a great deal of the information contained in the complete set of 230 historical relationships. An additional test, using a second set of 20 securities, gave similar results.

These results are, of course, far too fragmentary to be considered conclusive but they do suggest that the diagonal model may be able to represent the relationships among securities rather well and thus that the value of portfolio analyses based on the model will exceed their rather nominal cost. For these reasons it appears to be an excellent choice for the initial practical applications of the Markowitz technique.

References

1. Markowitz, Harry M., *Portfolio Selection, Efficient Diversification of Investments*, New York, John Wiley and Sons, Inc., 1959.

2. Markowitz, Harry M., "Portfolio Selection", *The Journal of Finance*, Vol. 12, (March 1952), 77–91.

3. Markowitz, Harry M., "The Optimization of a Quadratic Function Subject to Linear Constraints," *Naval Research Logistics Quarterly*, Vol. 3, (March and June, 1956), 111–133.

4. Wolfe, Philip, "The Simplex Method for Quadratic Programming," *Econometrica*, Vol. 27, (July, 1959), 382–398.

Capital Asset Prices: A Theory of Market Equilibrium under Conditions of Risk*

William F. Sharpe†

I.   Introduction

One of the problems which has plagued those attempting to predict the behavior of capital markets is the absence of a body of positive micro-economic theory dealing with conditions of risk. Although many useful insights can be obtained from the traditional models of investment under conditions of certainty, the pervasive influence of risk in financial transactions has forced those working in this area to adopt models of price behavior which are little more than assertions. A typical classroom explanation of the determination of capital asset prices, for example, usually begins with a careful and relatively rigorous description of the process through which individual preferences and physical relationships interact to determine an equilibrium pure interest rate. This is generally followed by the assertion that somehow a market risk-premium is also determined, with the prices of assets adjusting accordingly to account for differences in their risk.

A useful representation of the view of the capital market implied in such discussions is illustrated in Figure 1. In equilibrium, capital asset prices have

*A great many people provided comments on early versions of this paper which led to major improvements in the exposition. In addition to the referees, who were most helpful, the author wishes to express his appreciation to Dr. Harry Markowitz of the RAND Corporation, Professor Jack Hirshleifer of the University of California at Los Angeles, and to Professors Yoram Barzel, George Brabb, Bruce Johnson, Walter Oi and R. Haney Scott of the University of Washington.

†Associate Professor of Operations Research, University of Washington.

Reprinted from *The Journal of Finance* 19 (September 1964), pp. 425–442, by permission of the author and the publisher.

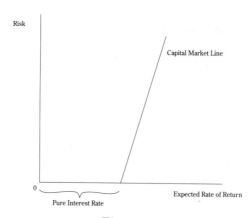

Figure 1

adjusted so that the investor, if he follows rational procedures (primarily diversification), is able to attain any desired point along a *capital market line*.[1] He may obtain a higher expected rate of return on his holdings only by incurring additional risk. In effect, the market presents him with two prices: the *price of time*, or the pure interest rate (shown by the intersection of the line with the horizontal axis) and the *price of risk*, the additional expected return per unit of risk borne (the reciprocal of the slope of the line).

At present there is no theory describing the manner in which the price of risk results from the basic influences of investor preferences, the physical attributes of capital assets, etc. Moreover, lacking such a theory, it is difficult to give any real meaning to the relationship between the price of a single asset and its risk. Through diversification, some of the risk inherent in an asset can be avoided so that its total risk is obviously not the relevant influence on its price; unfortunately little has been said concerning the particular risk component which is relevant.

In the last ten years a number of economists have developed *normative* models dealing with asset choice under conditions of risk. Markowitz,[2] following Von Neumann and Morgenstern, developed an analysis based on the expected utility maxim and proposed a general solution for the portfolio

---

[1]Although some discussions are also consistent with a non-linear (but monotonic) curve.

[2]Harry M. Markowitz, *Portfolio Selection, Efficient Diversification of Investments* (New York: John Wiley and Sons, Inc., 1959). The major elements of the theory first appeared in his article "Portfolio Selection," *The Journal of Finance*, XII (March 1952), 77–91.

selection problem. Tobin[3] showed that under certain conditions Markowitz's model implies that the process of investment choice can be broken down into two phases: first, the choice of a unique optimum combination of risky assets; and second, a separate choice concerning the allocation of funds between such a combination and a single riskless asset. Recently, Hicks[4] has used a model similar to that proposed by Tobin to derive corresponding conclusions about individual investor behavior, dealing somewhat more explicitly with the nature of the conditions under which the process of investment choice can be dichotomized. An even more detailed discussion of this process, including a rigorous proof in the context of a choice among lotteries has been presented by Gordon and Gangolli.[5]

Although all the authors cited use virtually the same model of investor behavior,[6] none has yet attempted to extend it to construct a *market* equilibrium theory of asset prices under conditions of risk.[7] We will show that such an extension provides a theory with implications consistent with the assertions of traditional financial theory described above. Moreover, it sheds considerable light on the relationship between the price of an asset and the various components of its overall risk. For these reasons it warrants consideration as a model of the determination of capital asset prices.

Part II provides the model of individual investor behavior under conditions of risk. In Part III the equilibrium conditions for the capital market are

---

[3]James Tobin, "Liquidity Preference as Behavior Towards Risk," *The Review of Economic Studies*, XXV (February, 1958), 65–86.

[4]John R. Hicks, "Liquidity," *The Economic Journal*, LXXII (December, 1962), 787–802.

[5]M. J. Gordon and Ramesh Gangolli, "Choice Among and Scale of Play on Lottery Type Alternatives," College of Business Administration, University of Rochester, 1962. For another discussion of this relationship see W. F. Sharpe, "A Simplified Model for Portfolio Analysis," *Management Science*, Vol. 9, No. 2 (January 1963), 277–293. A related discussion can be found in F. Modigliani and M. H. Miller, "The Cost of Capital, Corporation Finance, and the Theory of Investment," *The American Economic Review*, XLVIII (June 1958), 261–297.

[6]Recently Hirshleifer has suggested that the mean-variance approach used in the articles cited is best regarded as a special case of a more general formulation due to Arrow. See Hirshleifer's "Investment Decision Under Uncertainty," *Papers and Proceedings of the Seventy-Sixth Annual Meeting of the American Economic Association*, Dec. 1963, or Arrow's "Le Role des Valeurs Boursieres pour la Repartition la Meilleure des Risques," *International Colloquium on Econometrics*, 1952.

[7]After preparing this paper the author learned that Mr. Jack L. Treynor, of Arthur D. Little, Inc., had independently developed a model similar in many respects to the one described here. Unfortunately Mr. Treynor's excellent work on this subject is, at present, unpublished.

considered and the capital market line derived. The implications for the relationship between the prices of individual capital assets and the various components of risk are described in Part IV.

II.   Optimal Investment Policy for the Individual

The Investor's Preference Function

Assume that an individual views the outcome of any investment in probabilistic terms; that is, he thinks of the possible results in terms of some probability distribution. In assessing the desirability of a particular investment, however, he is willing to act on the basis of only two parameters of this distribution—its expected value and standard deviation.[8] This can be represented by a total utility function of the form:

$$U = f(E_w, \sigma_w)$$

where E_w indicates expected future wealth and σ_w the predicted standard deviation of the possible divergence of actual future wealth from E_w.

Investors are assumed to prefer a higher expected future wealth to a lower value, ceteris paribus ($dU/dE_w > 0$). Moreover, they exhibit risk-aversion, choosing an investment offering a lower value of σ_w to one with a greater level, given the level of E_w ($dU/d\sigma_w < 0$). These assumptions imply that indifference curves relating E_w and σ_w will be upward-sloping.[9]

To simplify the analysis, we assume that an investor has decided to commit a given amount (W_i) of his present wealth to investment. Letting W_t be his terminal wealth and R the rate of return on his investment:

$$R \equiv \frac{W_t - W_i}{W_i},$$

we have

$$W_t = RW_i + W_i.$$

---

[8]Under certain conditions the mean-variance approach can be shown to lead to unsatisfactory predictions of behavior. Markowitz suggests that a model based on the semi-variance (the average of the squared deviations below the mean) would be preferable; in light of the formidable computational problems, however, he bases his analysis on the variance and standard deviation.

[9]While only these characteristics are required for the analysis, it is generally assumed that the curves have the property of diminishing marginal rates of substitution between E_w and σ_w, as do those in our diagrams.

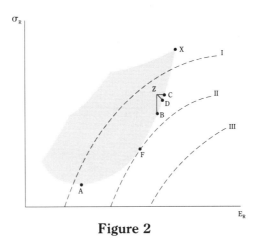

Figure 2

This relationship makes it possible to express the investor's utility in terms of R, since terminal wealth is directly related to the rate of return:

$$U = g(E_R, \sigma_R).$$

Figure 2 summarizes the model of investor preferences in a family of indifference curves; successive curves indicate higher levels of utility as one moves down and/or to the right. [10]

The Investment Opportunity Curve

The model of investor behavior considers the investor as choosing from a set of investment opportunities that one which maximizes his utility. Every invest-

---

[10] Such indifference curves can also be derived by assuming that the investor wishes to maximize expected utility and that his total utility can be represented by a quadratic function of R with decreasing marginal utility. Both Markowitz and Tobin present such a derivation. A similar approach is used by Donald E. Farrar in *The Investment Decision Under Uncertainty* (Prentice–Hall, 1962). Unfortunately Farrar makes an error in his derivation; he appeals to the Von-Neumann–Morgenstern cardinal utility axioms to transform a function of the form:

$$E(U) = a + bE_R - cE_R{}^2 - c\sigma_R{}^2$$

into one of the form:

$$E(U) = k_1 E_R - k_2 \sigma_R{}^2.$$

That such a transformation is not consistent with the axioms can readily be seen in this form, since the first equation implies non-linear indifference curves in the E_R, $\sigma_R{}^2$ plane while the second implies a linear relationship. Obviously no three (different) points can lie on both a line and a non-linear curve (with a monotonic derivative). Thus the two functions must imply different orderings among alternative choices in at least some instance.

ment plan available to him may be represented by a point in the E_R, σ_R plane. If all such plans involve some risk, the area composed of such points will have an appearance similar to that shown in Figure 2. The investor will choose from among all possible plans the one placing him on the indifference curve representing the highest level of utility (point F). The decision can be made in two stages: first, find the set of efficient investment plans, and second, choose one from among this set. A plan is said to be efficient if (and only if) there is no alternative with either (1) the same E_R and a lower σ_R, (2) the same σ_R and a higher E_R or (3) a higher E_R and a lower σ_R. Thus investment Z is inefficient since investments B, C, and D (among others) dominate it. The only plans which would be chosen must lie along the lower right-hand boundary ($AFBDCX$)—the *investment opportunity curve*.

To understand the nature of this curve, consider two investment plans—A and B, each including one or more assets. Their predicted expected values and standard deviations of rate of return are shown in Figure 3. If the proportion α of the individual's wealth is placed in plan A and the remainder $(1 - \alpha)$ in B, the expected rate of return of the combination will lie between The expected returns of the two plans:

$$E_{Rc} = \alpha E_{Ra} + (1 - \alpha)E_{Rb}$$

The predicted standard deviation of return of the combination is:

$$\sigma_{Rc} = \sqrt{\alpha^2 \sigma_{Ra}^2 + (1 - \alpha)^2 \sigma_{Rb}^2 + 2 r_{ab}\alpha(1 - \alpha)\sigma_{Ra}\sigma_{Rb}}$$

Note that this relationship includes r_{ab}, the correlation coefficient between the predicated rates of return of the two investment plans. A value of $+1$ would indicate an investor's belief that there is a precise positive relationship between the outcomes of the two investments. A zero value would indicate a belief that the outcomes of the two investments are completely independent and -1 that the investor feels that there is a precise inverse relationship between them. In the usual case r_{ab} will have a value between 0 and $+1$.

Figure 3 shows the possible values of E_{Rc} and σ_{Rc} obtainable with different combinations of A and B under two different assumptions about the value of r_{ab}. If the two investments are perfectly correlated, the combinations will lie along a straight line between the two points, since in this case both E_{Rc}

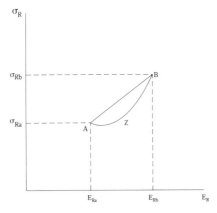

Figure 3

and σ_{Rc} will be linearly related to the proportions invested in the two plans. [11]
If they are less than perfectly positively correlated, the standard deviation of
any combination must be less than that obtained with perfect correlation (since
r_{ab} will be less); thus the combinations must lie along a curve below the line
AB. [12] AZB shows such a curve for the case of complete independence ($r_{ab} =$
0); with negative correlation the locus is even more U-shaped. [13]

The manner in which the investment opportunity curve is formed is
relatively simple conceptually, although exact solutions are usually quite

---

[11]
$$E_{Rc} = \alpha E_{Ra} + (1 - \alpha)E_{R_b} = E_{Rb} + (E_{R_a} - E_{R_b})\alpha$$

$$\sigma_{R_c} = \sqrt{\alpha^2 \sigma_{R_a}^2 + (1 - \alpha)^2 \sigma_{Rb}^2 + 2r_{ab}\,\alpha(1 - \alpha)\sigma_{Ra}\,\sigma_{Rb}}$$

but $r_{ab} = 1$, therefore the expression under the square root sign can be factored:

$$\sigma_{Rc} = \sqrt{[a\sigma_{Ra} + (1 - \alpha)\sigma_{R_b}]^2}$$

$$= \alpha\,\sigma_{Ra} + (1 - \alpha)\sigma_{Rb}$$

$$= \sigma_{Rb} + (\sigma_{Ra} - \sigma_{Rb})\alpha$$

[12] This curvature is, in essence, the rationale for diversification.

[13] When $r_{ab} = 0$, the slope of the curve at point A is $-\dfrac{\sigma_{Ra}}{E_{Rb} - E_{Ra}}$, at point B it is $\dfrac{\sigma_{Rb}}{E_{Rb} - E_{Ra}}$. When
$r_{ab} = -1$, the curve degenerates to two straight lines to a point on the horizontal axis.

difficult.[14] One first traces curves indicating E_R, σ_R values available with simple combinations of individual assets, then considers combinations of combinations of [*sic*] assets. The lower right-hand boundary must be either linear or increasing at an increasing rate ($d^2\sigma_R/dE^2_R > 0$). As suggested earlier, the complexity of the relationship between the characteristics of individual assets and the location of the investment opportunity curve makes it difficult to provide a simple rule for assessing the desirability of individual assets, since the effect of an asset on an investor's over-all investment opportunity curve depends not only on its expected rate of return (E_{Ri}) and risk (σ_{Ri}), but also on its correlations with the other available opportunities (r_{i1}, r_{i2}, ... , r_{in}). However, such a rule is implied by the equilibrium conditions for the model, as we will show in part IV.

The Pure Rate of Interest

We have not yet dealt with riskless assets. Let P be such an asset; its risk is zero ($\sigma_{Rp} = 0$) and its expected rate of return, E_{Rp}, is equal (by definition) to the pure interest rate. If an investor places α of his wealth in P and the remainder in some risky asset A, he would obtain an expected rate of return:

$$E_{Rc} = \alpha E_{Rp} + (1 - \alpha)E_{Ra}$$

The standard deviation of such a combination would be:

$$\sigma_{Rc} = \sqrt{\alpha^2 \sigma^2_{Rp} + (1 - \alpha)^2\sigma^2_{Ra} + 2r_{pa}\alpha(1 - \alpha)\sigma_{Rp}\sigma_{Ra}}$$

but since $\sigma_{Rp} = 0$, this reduces to:

$$\sigma_{Rc} = (1 - \alpha)\sigma_{Ra}.$$

This implies that all combinations involving any risky asset or combination of assets plus the riskless asset must have values of E_{Rc} and σ_{Rc} which lie along a straight line between the points representing the two components. Thus in Figure 4 all combinations of E_R and σ_R lying along the line PA are attainable if

---

[14]Markowitz has shown that this is a problem in parametric quadratic programming. An efficient solution technique is described in his article, "The Optimization of a Quadratic Function Subject to Linear Constraints," *Naval Research Logistics Quarterly*, Vol. 3 (March and June, 1956), 111–133. A solution method for a special case is given in the author's "A Simplified Model for Portfolio Analysis," *op. cit.*

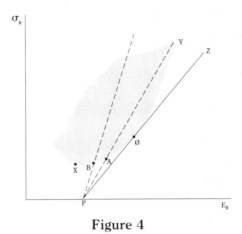

Figure 4

some money is loaned at the pure rate and some placed in A. Similarly, by lending at the pure rate and investing in B, combinations along PB can be attained. Of all such possibilities, however, one will dominate: that investment plan lying at the point of the original investment opportunity curve where a ray from point P is tangent to the curve. In Figure 4 all investments lying along the original curve from X to ϕ are dominated by some combination of investment in ϕ and lending at the pure interest rate.

Consider next the possibility of borrowing. If the investor can borrow at the pure rate of interest, this is equivalent to disinvesting in P. The effect of borrowing to purchase more of any given investment than is possible with the given amount of wealth can be found simply by letting α take on negative values in the equations derived for the case of lending. This will obviously give points lying along the extension of line PA if borrowing is used to purchase more of A; points lying along the extension of PB if the funds are used to purchase B, etc.

As in the case of lending, however, one investment plan will dominate all others when borrowing is possible. When the rate at which funds can be borrowed equals the lending rate, this plan will be the same one which is dominant if lending is to take place. Under these conditions, the investment opportunity curve becomes a line ($P\phi Z$ in Figure 4). Moreover, if the original investment opportunity curve is not linear at point ϕ, the process of investment choice can be dichotomized as follows: first select the (unique) optimum combination of risky assets (point ϕ), and second borrow or lend to obtain the particular point on PZ at which an indifference curve is tangent to the line. [15]

Before proceeding with the analysis, it may be useful to consider alternative assumptions under which only a combination of assets lying at the point of tangency between the original investment opportunity curve and a ray from P can be efficient. Even if borrowing is impossible, the investor will choose ϕ (and lending) if his risk-aversion leads him to a point below ϕ on the line $P\phi$. Since a large number of investors choose to place some of their funds in relatively risk-free investments, this is not an unlikely possibility. Alternatively, if borrowing is possible but only up to some limit, the choice of ϕ would be made by all but those investors willing to undertake considerable risk. These alternative paths lead to the main conclusion, thus making the assumption of borrowing or lending at the pure interest rate less onerous than it might initially appear to be.

III.   Equilibrium in the Capital Market

In order to derive conditions for equilibrium in the capital market we invoke two assumptions. First, we assume a common pure rate of interest, with all investors able to borrow or lend funds on equal terms. Second, we assume homogeneity of investor expectations: [16] investors are assumed to agree on the prospects of various investments—the expected values, standard deviations and correlation coefficients described in Part II. Needless to say, these are highly restrictive and undoubtedly unrealistic assumptions. However, since the proper test of a theory is not the realism of its assumptions but the acceptability of its implications, and since these assumptions imply equilibrium conditions which form a major part of classical financial doctrine, it is far from clear that this formulation should be rejected—especially in view of the dearth of alternative models leading to similar results.

Under these assumptions, given some set of capital asset prices, each

---

[15]This proof was first presented by Tobin for the case in which the pure rate of interest is zero (cash). Hicks considers the lending situation under comparable conditions but does not allow borrowing. Both authors present their analysis using maximization subject to constraints expressed as equalities. Hicks' analysis assumes independence and thus insures that the solution will include no negative holdings of risky assets; Tobin's covers the general case, thus his solution would generally include negative holdings of some assets. The discussion in this paper is based on Markowitz' formulation, which includes non-negativity constraints on the holdings of all assets.

[16]A term suggested by one of the referees.

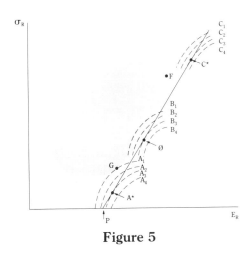

Figure 5

investor will view his alternatives in the same manner. For one set of prices the alternatives might appear as shown in Figure 5. In this situation, an investor with the preferences indicated by indifference curves A_1 through A_4 would seek to lend some of his funds at the pure interest rate and to invest the remainder in the combination of assets shown by point ϕ, since this would give him the preferred over-all position A^*. An investor with the preferences indicated by curves B_1 through B_4 would seek to invest all his funds in combination ϕ, while an investor with indifference curves C_1 through C_4 would invest all his funds plus additional (borrowed) funds in combination ϕ in order to reach his preferred position (C^*). In any event, all would attempt to purchase only those risky assets which enter combination ϕ.

The attempts by investors to purchase the assets in combination ϕ and their lack of interest in holding assets not in combination ϕ would, of course, lead to a revision of prices. The prices of assets in ϕ will rise and, since an asset's expected return relates future income to present price, their expected returns will fall. This will reduce the attractiveness of combinations which include such assets; thus point ϕ (among others) will move to the left of its initial position. [17] On the other hand, the prices of assets not in ϕ will fall, causing an increase in their expected returns and a rightward movement of points representing combinations which include them. Such price changes will lead to

---

[17] If investors consider the variability of future dollar returns unrelated to present price, both E_R and σ_R will fall; under these conditions the point representing an asset would move along a ray through the origin as its price changes.

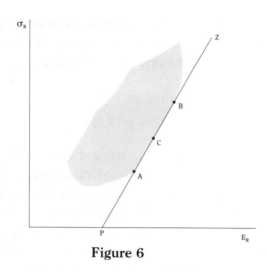

Figure 6

a revision of investors' actions; some new combination or combinations will become attractive, leading to different demands and thus to further revisions in prices. As the process continues, the investment opportunity curve will tend to become more linear, with points such as ϕ moving to the left and formerly inefficient points (such as F and G) moving to the right.

Capital asset prices must, of course, continue to change until a set of prices is attained for which every asset enters at least one combination lying on the capital market line. Figure 6 illustrates such an equilibrium condition. [18] All possibilities in the shaded area can be attained with combinations of risky assets, while points lying along the line PZ can be attained by borrowing or lending at the pure rate plus an investment in some combination of risky assets. Certain possibilities (those lying along PZ from point A to point B) can be obtained in either manner. For example, the E_R, σ_R values shown by point A can be obtained solely by some combination of risky assets; alternatively, the point can be reached by a combination of lending and investing in combination C of risky assets.

It is important to recognize that in the situation shown in Figure 6 many alternative combinations of risky assets are efficient (i.e., lie along line PZ), and thus the theory does not imply that all investors will hold the same combina-

---

[18]The area in Figure 6 representing E_R, σ_R values attained with only risky assets has been drawn at some distance from the horizontal axis for emphasis. It is likely that a more accurate representation would place it very close to the axis.

tion.[19] On the other hand, all such combinations must be perfectly (positively) correlated, since they lie along a linear border of the E_R, σ_R region.[20] This provides a key to the relationship between the prices of capital assets and different types of risk.

IV.   The Prices of Capital Assets

We have argued that in equilibrium there will be a simple linear relationship between the expected return and standard deviation of return for efficient combinations of risky assets. Thus far nothing has been said about such a relationship for individual assets. Typically the E_R, σ_R values associated with single assets will lie above the capital market line, reflecting the inefficiency of undiversified holdings. Moreover, such points may be scattered throughout the feasible region, with no consistent relationship between their expected return and total risk (σ_R). However, there will be a consistent relationship between their expected returns and what might best be called *systematic risk*, as we will now show.

Figure 7 illustrates the typical relationship between a single capital asset (point i) and an efficient combination of assets (point g) of which it is a part. The curve *igg'* indicates all E_R, σ_R values which can be obtained with feasible combinations of asset i and combination g. As before, we denote such a combination in terms of a proportion α of asset i and $(1 - \alpha)$ of combination g. A value of $\alpha = 1$ would indicate pure investment in asset i while $\alpha = 0$ would imply investment in combination g. Note, however, that $\alpha = .5$ implies a total investment of more than half the funds in asset i, since half would be invested in i itself and the other half used to purchase combination g, which also includes some of asset i. This means that a combination in which asset i does not appear

---

[19]This statement contradicts Tobin's conclusion that there will be a unique optimal combination of risky assets. Tobin's proof of a unique optimum can be shown to be incorrect for the case of perfect correlation of efficient risky investment plans if the line connecting their E_R, σ_R points would pass through point P. In the graph on page 83 of this article (*op. cit.*) the constant-risk locus would, in this case, degenerate from a family of ellipses into one of straight lines parallel to the constant-return loci, thus giving multiple optima.

[20]E_R, σ_R values given by combinations of any two combinations must lie within the region and cannot plot above a straight line joining the points. In this case they cannot plot below such a straight line. But since only in the case of perfect correlation will they plot along a straight line, the two combinations must be perfectly correlated. As shown in Part IV, this does not necessarily imply that the individual securities they contain are perfectly correlated.

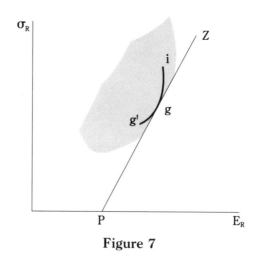

Figure 7

at all must be represented by some negative value of α. Point g' indicates such a combination.

In Figure 7 the curve igg' has been drawn tangent to the capital market line (PZ) at point g. This is no accident. All such curves must be tangent to the capital market line in equilibrium, since (1) they must touch it at the point representing the efficient combination and (2) they are continuous at that point.[21] Under these conditions a lack of tangency would imply that the curve intersects PZ. But then some feasible combination of assets would lie to the right of the capital market line, an obvious impossibility since the capital market line represents the efficient boundary of feasible values of E_R and σ_R.

The requirement that curves such as igg' be tangent to the capital market line can be shown to lead to a relatively simple formula which relates the expected rate of return to various elements of risk for all assets which are included in combination g.[22] Its economic meaning can best be seen if the

---

[21] Only if $r_{ig} = -1$ will the curve be discontinuous over the range in question.

[22] The standard deviation of a combination of g and i will be:

$$\sigma = \sqrt{\alpha^2 \sigma_{Ri}{}^2 + (1-\alpha)^2 \sigma_{Rg}{}^2 + 2r_{ig}\alpha(1-\alpha)\sigma_{Ri}\sigma_{Rg}}$$

at $\alpha = 0$:

$$\frac{d\sigma}{d\alpha} = -\frac{1}{\sigma}[\sigma_{Rg}{}^2 - r_{ig}\,\sigma_{Ri}\,\sigma_{Rg}]$$

but $\sigma = \sigma_{Rg}$ at $\alpha = 0$. Thus:

relationship between the return of asset i and that of combination g is viewed in a manner similar to that used in regression analysis. [23] Imagine that we were given a number of (ex post) observations of the return of the two investments. The points might plot as shown in Fig. 8. The scatter of the R_i observations around their mean (which will approximate E_{Ri}) is, of course, evidence of the total risk of the asset—σ_{Ri}. But part of the scatter is due to an underlying relationship with the return on combination g, shown by B_{ig}, the slope of the regression line. The response of R_i to changes in R_g (and variations in R_g itself) account for much of the variation in R_i. It is this component of the asset's total

$$\frac{d\sigma}{d\alpha} = -[\sigma_{Rg} - r_{ig}\,\sigma_{Ri}]$$

The expected return of a combination will be:

$$E = \alpha E_{Ri} + (1 - \alpha)E_{Rg}$$

Thus, at all values of α:

$$\frac{dE}{d\alpha} = -[E_{Rg} - E_{Ri}]$$

and, at $\alpha = 0$:

$$\frac{d\sigma}{dE} = \frac{\sigma_{Rg} - r_{ig}\,\sigma_{Ri}}{E_{Rg} - E_{Ri}}.$$

Let the equation of the capital market line be:

$$\sigma_R = s(E_R - P)$$

where P is the pure interest rate. Since igg' is tangent to the line when $\alpha = 0$, and since (E_{Rg}, σ_{Rg}) lies on the line:

$$\frac{\sigma_{Rg} - r_{ig}\,\sigma_{Ri}}{E_{Rg} - E_{Ri}} = \frac{\sigma_{Rg}}{E_{Rg} - P}$$

or:

$$\frac{r_{ig}\,\sigma_{Ri}}{\sigma_{Rg}} = -\left[\frac{P}{E_{Rg} - P}\right] + \left[\frac{1}{E_{Rg} - P}\right] E_{Ri}.$$

[23]This model has been called the diagonal model since its portfolio analysis solution can be facilitated by re-arranging the data so that the variance-covariance matrix becomes diagonal. The method is described in the author's article, cited earlier.

risk which we term the *systematic risk*. The remainder,[24] being uncorrelated with R_g, is the unsystematic component. This formulation of the relationship between R_i and R_g can be employed *ex ante* as a predictive model. B_{ig} becomes the *predicted* response of R_i to changes in R_g. Then, given σ_{Rg} (the predicted risk of R_g), the systematic portion of the predicted risk of each asset can be determined.

This interpretation allows us to state the relationship derived from the tangency of curves such as *igg'* with the capital market line in the form shown in Figure 9. All assets entering efficient combination g must have (predicted) B_{ig} and E_{Ri} values lying on the line PQ.[25] Prices will adjust so that assets which are more responsive to changes in R_g will have higher expected returns than those which are less responsive. This accords with common sense. Obviously the part of an asset's risk which is due to its correlation with the return on a combination cannot be diversified away when the asset is added to the combination. Since B_{ig} indicates the magnitude of this type of risk it should be directly related to expected return.

The relationship illustrated in Figure 9 provides a partial answer to the question posed earlier concerning the relationship between an asset's risk and its expected return. But thus far we have argued only that the relationship holds for the assets which enter some particular efficient combination (g). Had another combination been selected, a different linear relationship would have been derived. Fortunately this limitation is easily overcome. As shown in the

---

[24] ex post, the standard error.

[25]
$$r_{ig} = \sqrt{\frac{B_{ig}^2 \sigma_{Rg}^2}{\sigma_{Ri}^2}} = \frac{B_{ig} \sigma_{Rg}}{\sigma_{Ri}}$$

and:

$$B_{ig} = \frac{r_{ig} \sigma_{Ri}}{\sigma_{Rg}}.$$

The expression on the right is the expression on the left-hand side of the last equation in footnote 22. Thus:

$$B_{ig} = -\left[\frac{P}{E_{Rg} - P}\right] + \left[\frac{1}{E_{Rg} - P}\right] E_{Ri}.$$

footnote, [26] we may arbitrarily select *any* one of the efficient combinations, then measure the predicted responsiveness of *every* asset's rate of return to that of the combination selected; and these coefficients will be related to the expected rates of return of the assets in exactly the manner pictured in Figure 9.

The fact that rates of return from all efficient combinations will be

---

[26] Consider the two assets i and i^*, the former included in efficient combination g and the latter in combination g^*. As shown above:

$$B_{ig} = -\left[\frac{P}{E_{Rg} - P}\right] + \left[\frac{1}{E_{Rg} - P}\right]E_{Ri}$$

and:

$$B_{i^*g^*} = -\left[\frac{P}{E_{Rg^*} - P}\right] + \left[\frac{1}{E_{Rg^*} - P}\right]E_{Ri^*}.$$

Since R_g and R_{g^*} are perfectly correlated:

$$r_{i^*g^*} = r_{i^*g}$$

Thus:

$$\frac{B_{i^*g^*}\,\sigma_{Rg^*}}{\sigma_{Ri^*}} = \frac{B_{i^*g}\,\sigma_{Rg}}{\sigma_{Ri^*}}$$

and:

$$B_{i^*g^*} = B_{i^*g}\left[\frac{\sigma_{Rg}}{\sigma_{Rg^*}}\right].$$

Since both g and g^* lie on a line which intercepts the E-axis at P:

$$\frac{\sigma_{Rg}}{\sigma_{Rg^*}} = \frac{E_{Rg} - P}{E_{Rg^*} - P}$$

and:

$$B_{i^*g^*} = B_{i^*g}\left[\frac{E_{Rg} - P}{E_{Rg^*} - P}\right]$$

Thus:

$$-\left[\frac{P}{E_{Rg^*} - P}\right] + \left[\frac{1}{E_{Rg^*} - P}\right]E_{Ri^*} = B_{i^*g}\left[\frac{E_{Rg} - P}{E_{Rg^*} - P}\right]$$

from which we have the desired relationship between R_{i^*} and g:

$$B_{i^*g} = -\left[\frac{P}{E_{Rg} - P}\right] + \left[\frac{1}{E_{Rg} - P}\right]E_{Ri^*}$$

B_{i^*g} must therefore plot on the same line as does B_{ig}.

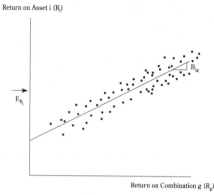

Figure 8

perfectly correlated provides the justification for arbitrarily selecting any one of them. Alternatively we may choose instead any variable perfectly correlated with the rate of return of such combinations. The vertical axis in Figure 9 would then indicate alternative levels of a coefficient measuring the sensitivity of the rate of return of a capital asset to changes in the variable chosen.

This possibility suggests both a plausible explanation for the implication that all efficient combinations will be perfectly correlated and a useful interpretation of the relationship between an individual asset's expected return and its risk. Although the theory itself implies only that rates of return from efficient combinations will be perfectly correlated, we might expect that this would be due to their common dependence on the over-all level of economic activity. If so, diversification enables the investor to escape all but the risk resulting from

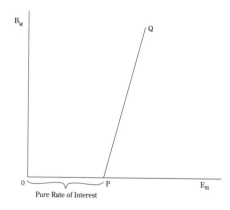

Figure 9

swings in economic activity—this type of risk remains even in efficient combinations. And, since all other types can be avoided by diversification, only the responsiveness of an asset's rate of return to the level of economic activity is relevant in assessing its risk. Prices will adjust until there is a linear relationship between the magnitude of such responsiveness and expected return. Assets which are unaffected by changes in economic activity will return the pure interest rate; those which move with economic activity will promise appropriately higher expected rates of return.

This discussion provides an answer to the second of the two questions posed in this paper. In Part III it was shown that with respect to equilibrium conditions in the capital market as a whole, the theory leads to results consistent with classical doctrine (i.e., the capital market line). We have now shown that with regard to capital assets considered individually, it also yields implications consistent with traditional concepts: it is common practice for investment counselors to accept a lower expected return from defensive securities (those which respond little to changes in the economy) than they require from aggressive securities (which exhibit significant response). As suggested earlier, the familiarity of the implications need not be considered a drawback. The provision of a logical framework for producing some of the major elements of traditional financial theory should be a useful contribution in its own right.

Nobel Lecture

December 7, 1990

Leverage

Merton H. Miller

Robert R. McCormick Distinguished Service Professor
Graduate School of Business
University of Chicago

1.0   Introduction

Under the terms of Alfred Nobel's will, the Prizes were to be awarded for an "important discovery or invention." Let it be clear from the outset, therefore, that my case must be one of the former, not the latter. Contrary to what you may have read in some press accounts following the announcement of the 1990 Nobel Prizes in Economic Sciences, I am not the co-inventor of the leveraged buyout—the transaction that perhaps more than any other has come to symbolize the supposed financial excesses of the 1980's. Leveraged buyouts (LBO's), in which the younger, active managers of a firm borrowed the funds to buy the controlling shares from a firm's retired founder (or from his estate) were an established feature of the corporate landscape long before Franco Modigliani, the 1985 laureate, and I published our first joint paper on leverage and the cost of capital in 1958. The LBO's of the 1980's differed only in scale, in that they involved publicly-held rather than privately-held corporations and in that the takeovers were often hostile.

That Franco Modigliani and I should be credited with inventing these takeovers is doubly ironic since the central message of our M&M Propositions was that the value of the firm was independent of its capital structure. Subject to one important qualification to be duly noted below, you couldn't hope to enhance shareholder value merely by leveraging up. Investors would not pay a premium for corporate leverage because they could always leverage up their own holdings by borrowing on personal account. Despite this seemingly clear prediction of the M&M analysis, the LBO's of the 1980's were routinely reporting premiums to the shareholders of more than 40 percent, running in some cases as high as 100 percent and all this, mind you even after the huge fees the deal-making investment bankers were extracting.

The qualification to the M&M value-invariance proposition mentioned earlier concerns the deductibility of interest payments under the unintegrated U.S. corporate income tax. That deductibility can lead, as we showed in our 1963 article, to substantial gains from leveraging under some conditions, and gains of this tax-driven kind have undoubtedly figured both in the rise of corporate debt ratios generally in the 1980's and in some recent LBO's and voluntary restructurings in particular. But after netting out the offsetting tax costs of leveraged capital structures (such as those discussed in my paper "Debt and Taxes" (1977) and its follow-up literature), tax savings alone cannot plausibly account for the observed LBO premiums.

1.1 Leveraged buyouts: where the gains came from

The source of the major gains in value achieved in the LBO's of the 1980's lies, in fact, not in our newly-recognized field of finance at all, but in that older, and long-established field of economics, industrial organization. Perhaps industrial *re*organization might be an apter term. Mikhail Gorbachev, the 1990 Peace Prize Winner, may have popularized the term *perestroika*, but the LBO entrepreneurs of the 1980's actually did it, and on a scale not seen since the early years of this century when so much of what we think of as big business was being put together by the entrepreneurs of consolidation like J.P. Morgan and John D. Rockefeller.

That the LBO entrepreneurs have achieved substantial real efficiency gains by reconcentrating corporate control and redeploying assets has been amply documented in a multitude of academic research studies. (See Kaplan (1989).) But this basically positive view of LBO's and takeovers is still far from universally accepted among the wider public. Some are reacting to the layoffs and factory closings that have sometimes followed hostile takeovers, although far more of both have occurred in our automobile industry which has so far been immune from takeovers. Others worry that these short-run gains may represent merely the improvident sacrifice of opportunities for high, but long deferred future profits—an argument presuming among other things, that the market cannot properly compute discounted present values. Even more fear that the real efficiency gains, if any, will be more than offset by the collateral damage from the financial leveraging used to bring about the restructuring.

1.2   The problems of corporate leveraging: real or imagined?

These fears will be the main focus of this lecture. The statutes of the Nobel Foundation stipulate that the subject of the Nobel Lecture "should be on or associated with the work for which the prize was awarded," which, in my case means the M&M propositions. Rather than simply reviewing them, however, or discussing the subsequent research they have inspired (a task already undertaken in Miller (1988)) I propose here instead to show how those propositions bear on current concerns about overleveraging—concerns that in some quarters actually border on hysteria. In particular I will argue, first, that the highly visible losses and defaults on junk bonds do not mean that overleveraging did in fact occur; second, paradoxical as it may sound, that increased leveraging by corporations does not imply increased risk for the economy as a whole; third, that the financial distress being suffered by some highly leveraged firms involves mainly private, not social costs; and finally, that the capital markets have built-in controls against overleveraging—controls, moreover, very much in evidence at the moment. Recent efforts by our regulators to override these built-in market mechanisms by destroying the junk bond market and by imposing additional direct controls over leveraged lending by banks will thus have all the unintended consequences normally associated with such regulatory interventions. They will lower efficiency and raise costs (in this case, the cost of capital) to important sectors of our economy.

That the current emphasis on the evils of overleveraging may be misplaced does not mean, of course, that all is well. My message is not: "Relax. Be happy. And, don't worry." Worry we should, in the U.S. at least, but about the serious problems confronting us, such as our seeming inability to bring government spending under rational control or to halt the steady deterioration of our once-vaunted system of public education. Let us not waste our limited worrying capacity on second-order and largely self-correcting problems like financial leveraging.

I hope I will be pardoned for dwelling in what follows almost exclusively on U.S. examples. It's just that a particularly virulent strain of the anti-leverage hysteria seems to have struck us first. Perhaps others can learn from our mistakes.

2.0 The Private and Social Costs of Corporate Leveraging

The charge that the U.S. became overleveraged in the 1980's will strike some as perhaps too obvious to require any extensive documentation. What could offer more compelling evidence of the over issuance of debt than the defaults of so many junk-bond issuers in late 1989, with news of additional or pending defaults now almost a daily occurrence?

2.1 The junk bonds as just another risky security

To argue in this all too natural way, however, is to put too much emphasis on the word "bond" and not enough on the word "junk." Bonds are, indeed, promises to pay. And certainly the issuers of the bonds hoped to keep those promises. But if the firm's cash flow, for reasons competitive or cyclical, fails to cover the commitments, then the promises cannot be kept, or at least not kept in full.

The buyers of the junk bonds, of course, also *hoped* that the promises would be kept. But they clearly weren't counting on it! For all save the most hopelessly gullible, the yields *expected* (in the Markowitz sense of yield outcomes weighted by probability of occurrence) on junk bonds, were below the nominal or promised yields. The high promised yields that might be earned during the good years were understood as compensation for the possible bad years in time and bad bonds in the total junk bond portfolio. The high nominal yields, in short, were essentially risk premiums. And in 1989, for many of the junk bonds issued earlier, the risk happened.

Although the presumption in finance is that defaults represent bad outcomes *ex post*, rather than systematic misperception of the true *ex ante* odds, as seems to be the conventional view, that presumption cannot yet be established conclusively. The time series of rates of return on junk bonds is still too short for judging whether those returns are indeed anomalously too low (or perhaps even anomalously too high) relative to accepted asset-pricing models like those of my co-laureate William Sharpe and his successors. Few such anomalous asset classes have so far been identified; and nothing in the nature of high-yield bonds strongly suggests that they will wind up on that short list.

Some may question the fairness of my treating these realized risks on junk bonds as essentially exogenous shocks, like earthquakes or droughts. Surely, they would contend, the very rise of corporate leverage that the junk bonds represent must itself have increased the total risk in the economy. On that point, however, modern finance in general and the M&M propositions in particular offer a different and in many respects, a counter-intuitive perspective.

2.2   Does increased corporate leverage add to society's risk?

Imagine that you, as a venerable academic professor of finance are in a dialogue with an equally grizzled corporate treasurer who believes, as most of them probably do, that leveraging *does* increase total risk. "You will surely concede, Professor," he is likely to begin, "that leveraging up the corporate capital structure will make the remaining equity riskier. Right?" "Right," you say. A company with a debt/equity ratio of 1, for example, earning a 20 percent rate of return on its underlying assets and paying 10 percent on its bonds, which, of course, have the first claim on the firm's earnings, will generate an enhanced 30 percent rate of return for its equity holders. Should the earning rate on the underlying assets decline by 25 percent, however, to 15 percent, the rate of return on equity will fall by an even greater extent (33 1/3 percent in this case). That, after all, is why we use the graphic term leverage (or the equally descriptive term gearing that the British seem to prefer). And this greater variability of prospective rates of return to leveraged shareholders means greater risk, in precisely the sense used by my colleagues here, Harry Markowitz and William Sharpe.

That conceded, the corporate treasurer goes on to ask rhetorically: "And, Professor, any debt added to the capital structure must, necessarily, be riskier debt, carrying a lower rating and bearing a higher interest rate than on any debt outstanding before the higher leveraging. Right?" "Right," you again agree, and for exactly the same reason as before. The further a claimant stands from the head of the line at payoff time, the riskier the claim.

Now the treasurer moves in for the kill. "Leveraging raises the risk of the equity and also raises the risk of the debt. It must, therefore, raise the total risk. Right?" "Wrong," you say, preparing to play the M&M card. The M&M propositions are the finance equivalents of conservation laws. What gets conserved in this case is the risk of the earning stream generated by the firm's operating assets. Leveraging or deleveraging the firm's capital structure serves merely to partition that risk among the firm's security holders. [1]

To see where the risk goes, consider the following illustrative example. Suppose a firm has 10 security holders of whom 5 hold the firm's bonds and the remaining 5 hold equal shares in the firm's leveraged equity. Suppose further that the interest due on the 5 bonds is covered sufficiently for those bonds to be considered essentially riskless. The entire risk of the firm must thus be borne by the 5 shareholders who will, of course, expect a rate of return on their investment substantially higher than on the assumed riskless bonds. Let 2 of the common stockholders now come to feel that their share of the risks is higher than they want to bear. They ask to exchange their stockholdings for bonds, but they learn that the interest payments on the 2 additional bonds they will get in exchange could not be covered in all possible states of the world. To avoid diluting the claims of the old bondholders, the new bonds must be made junior to the old bonds. Because the new bonds are riskier, the 2 new bondholders will expect a rate of return higher than on the old riskless bonds, but a rate still less, of course, than on their original, and even higher-risk holdings of common stock. The *average* risk and the average expected interest rate of the 7 bondholders taken together has thus risen. At the same time, the risk assumed by the remaining 3 equity holders is also higher (since the 2 shifting stockholders now have taken a prior claim on the firm's earnings) and their expected return must rise as well. Both classes of securities are thus riskier on average, but the *total* risk stays exactly the same as before the 2 stockholders shifted over. The increased risk to the 3 remaining stockholders is exactly offset by decreased risk to the 2 former stockholders who have moved down the priority ladder to become junior bondholders. [2]

---

[1] In the original M&M paper, that underlying real earning stream was taken as a given, independent of the financing decisions. Subsequent research has identified many possible interactions between the real and the financial sides of the firm, but their effects on risk are not always in the same direction and for present purposes, they can be regarded as of only second-order importance.

[2] Note, incidentally, that this story would have exactly the same conclusion if the 2 defecting common stockholders had opted for preferred stocks rather than junior bonds. Even though accountants classify preferred stocks as equity, preferreds are functionally equivalent to junior debt. Preferred stocks, in fact, were effectively the junk bonds of finance (often with the same bad press) prior to the 1930's when the steep rise in corporate tax rates made them less attractive than tax-deductible, interest-bearing securities of equivalent priority.

2.3   Leverage and the deadweight costs of financial distress

That aggregate risk might be unaffected by modest changes of leverage some might willingly concede, but not when leverage is pushed to the point that bankruptcy becomes a real possibility. The higher the leverage, the greater the likelihood, of course, that just such an unfortunate event will occur.

Actually, however, the M&M conservation of risk continues to hold, subject to some qualifications to be duly noted below, even in the extreme case of default. That result seems paradoxical only because the emotional and psychological overtones of the word bankruptcy give that particular outcome more prominence than it merits on strictly economic grounds. From a bloodless finance perspective, a default signifies merely that the stockholders have now lost their entire stake in the firm. Their option, so to speak, has expired worthless. The creditors now become the new stockholders and the return on their original debt claims becomes whatever of value is left in the firm.

The qualification to the principle of risk conservation noted earlier is that the very process of transferring claims from the debtors to the creditors can itself create risks and deadweight costs over and beyond those involved when the firm was a going concern. Some of these "costs of financial distress," as they have come to be called, may be incurred even before a default occurs. Debtors, like some poets, do not "go gentle into that good night." They struggle to keep their firms alive, even if sometimes the firm would be better off dead by any rational calculation. They are often assisted in those efforts at life-support by a bankruptcy code that materially strengthens their hands in negotiations with the creditors. Sometimes, of course, the reverse can happen and over-rapacious creditors can force liquidation of firms that might otherwise have survived. About all we can safely conclude is that once the case is in bankruptcy court, all sides in these often-protracted negotiations will be assisted by armies of lawyers whose fees further eat away the pool of assets available to satisfy the claims of the creditors. For small firms, the direct costs of the bankruptcy proceedings can easily consume the entire corpus (an apt term), but they are essentially fixed costs and hence represent only a small portion of the recoveries in the larger cases. In the aggregate, of course, direct bankruptcy costs, even if regarded as complete social waste, are minuscule relative to the size of the economy. [3]

---

[3]The deadweight costs of bankruptcy, and of financial distress more generally, may be small in the aggregate, but they do exist. A case can be made, therefore, on standard welfare-economics grounds for eliminating the

2.4   The costs of financial distress: private or social?

Small as the aggregate deadweight costs of financial distress may be, bankruptcies can certainly be painful personal tragedies. Even so generally unadmired a public figure as Donald Trump has almost become an object of public sympathy as he struggles with his creditors for control over his garish Taj Mahal Casino. But even if he does lose, as seemed probable at the time of this writing, the loss will be his, not society's. The Trump casino and associated buildings will still be there (perhaps one should add, alas). The only difference will be the sign on the door: Under New Management. [4]

The social consequences of the isolated bankruptcy can be dismissed perhaps, but not, some would argue, bankruptcies that come in clusters. The fear is that the bankruptcy of each overindebted firm will send a shock wave to the firm's equally overindebted suppliers leading in turn to more bankruptcies until eventually the whole economy collapses in a heap. Neither economics generally nor finance in particular, however, offer much support for this notion of a leverage-induced "bankruptcy multiplier" or a contagion effect. Bankrupt firms, as noted earlier, do not vanish from the earth. They often continue operating pretty much as before, though with different ownership and possibly on a reduced scale. Even when they do liquidate and close down, their inventory, furniture and fixtures, employees and their customers flow to other firms elsewhere in the economy. Profitable investment opportunities that one failing firm passes up will be assumed by others, if not always immediately, then later when the economic climate becomes more favorable. Recent research in macro-economics suggests that much of what we used to consider as output irretrievably lost in business cycles is really only output postponed, particularly in the durable goods industries.

To say that the human and capital resources of bankrupt firms will eventually be reemployed, is not to deny, of course, that the personal costs of disemployment merit consideration, particularly when they become wide-

---

current tax subsidy to debt implicit in our current unintegrated corporate income tax. Achieving complete neutrality between debt and equity, however, would require elimination of the corporate tax—a step not likely to be undertaken in the foreseeable future.

[4] Actually, according to recent press reports, Trump's creditors have allowed him to keep control, at least temporarily. Should he fail to meet stipulated cash-flow targets, however, the creditors can take over his remaining interests in a so-called "pre-packaged" bankruptcy, that is, one without formal bankruptcy proceedings (and expenses). Further use of this ingenious and efficient method for transferring control can confidently be expected.

spread. All modern economies take steps to ease the pains of transferring human resources to other and better uses, and perhaps they should do even more. But delaying or preventing the needed movements of resources will also have social costs that can be even higher over the long run as the economies of Eastern Europe are discovering.

The successive waves of bankruptcies in the early 1930's may seem to belie this relatively benign view of bankruptcy as a matter essentially of private costs with no serious externalities, but not really. [5] Contrary to widely-held folk beliefs, bankruptcies did not bring on the Great Depression. The direction of causation runs from depressions to bankruptcies, not the other way around. The collapse of the stock market in 1929 and of the U.S. banking system during 1931–2 may well have created the appearance of a finance-driven disaster. But that disaster was not just the inevitable bursting of another overleveraged tulip bubble as some have suggested. (Actually recent research has cast doubt on the existence of even the *original* tulip bubble. But that is another story. See Garber (1989).) Responsibility for turning an ordinary downturn into a depression of unprecedented severity lies primarily with the managers of the Federal Reserve System. They failed to carry out their duties as the residual supplier of liquidity to the public and to the banking system. The U.S. money supply imploded by 30 percent between 1930 and 1932, dragging the economy and the price level down with it. When that happens even AAA credits get to look like junk bonds.

That such a nightmare scenario might be repeated under present day conditions is always possible, of course, but, until recently at least, most economists would have dismissed it as extremely unlikely. The current chairman of the Federal Reserve Board himself, as well as his staff, are known to have studied the dismal episode of the early 1930's in great depth and to be thoroughly aware of how and why their ill-fated predecessors had blundered. The prompt action by the Federal Reserve Board to support the liquidity of the banking system after the stock market crash of October 19, 1987 (and again after the mini-crash of October 13, 1989) is testimony to the lessons learned. The fear of some at the moment, however, is that both the willingness and the ability of the Federal Reserve to maintain the economy's liquidity and its credit

---

[5]True externalities arise, as in the case of air pollution, only when actions by one firm increase the costs of others. A possible analog to pollution for corporate debt might be the shifting to the government and hence to the taxpayers, of the pension costs of failed firms. Once again, however, the aggregate impact is of only second-order significance.

system are being undermined by regulatory overreaction to the S&L crisis—an overreaction that stems in part from underestimating the market's internal controls on overleveraging.

3.0   The Self-Correcting Tendencies in Corporate Leveraging

Just what combination of demand shifts and supply shifts triggered the big expansion in leveraged securities in the 1980's will eventually have to be sorted out by future economic historians. The main point to be emphasized here is that whether we are talking automobiles or leveraged equity or high-yield bonds the market's response to changes in tastes (or to changes in production technology) is limited and self-regulating. If the producers of any commodity expand its supply faster than the buyers want, the price will fall and output eventually will shrink. And similarly, in the financial markets. If the public's demand for junk bonds is overestimated by takeover entrepreneurs, the higher interest rates they must offer to junk-bond buyers will eat into the gains from the deals. The process of further leveraging will slow and perhaps even be reversed.

Something very much like this endogenous slowing of leveraging could be discerned in early 1989 even before a sequence of government initiatives (including the criminal indictments of the leading investment bankers and market makers in junk bonds, the forced dumping of junk bond inventories by beleaguered S&L's and the stricter regulations on leveraged lending by commercial banks) combined to undermine the liquidity of the high-yield bond market. The issuance of high-yield bonds not only ground to a halt, but many highly-leveraged firms moved to replace their now high-cost debts with equity. [6]

3.1   Junk bonds and the S&L crisis

To point out that the market has powerful endogenous controls against overleveraging does not mean that who holds the highly leveraged securities is never a matter of concern. Certainly the U.S. Savings and Loan Institutions should not have been using government-guaranteed savings deposits to buy high-risk junk bonds. But to focus so much attention on the junk bond losses of

---

[6]The process of swapping equity for debt (essentially the reverse of the parable in Section 2.2) would have gone even further by now but for an unfortunate feature of U.S. tax law. Swapping equity for debt selling at less than face value creates taxable income from "cancellation of indebtedness." An exception is made for firms in bankruptcy making that option more attractive than it otherwise might be for firms whose debts are at a sizeable discount.

a handful of these S&L's is to miss the main point of that whole sorry episode. The current hue and cry over S&L junk bonds serves merely to divert attention from those who expanded the government deposit guarantees and encouraged the S&L's to make investments with higher expected returns, but alas, also with higher risk than their traditional long-term home mortgages.

Some, at the time, defended the enlargement of the government's deposit guarantee as compensation for the otherwise disabling interest rate risks assumed by those undertaking the socially-desirable task of providing fixed rate, long-term mortgages. Quite apart, however, from the presence even then of alternative and less vulnerable ways of supplying mortgage money, the deposit guarantees proved to be, as most finance specialists had predicted at the time, a particularly unfortunate form of subsidy to home ownership. Because the deposit guarantees gave the owners of the S&L's what amounted to put options against the government, they actually encouraged the undertaking of uneconomic long-odds projects, some of which made junk bonds look safe by comparison. The successes went to the owners; the failures, to the insurance fund.

More is at stake, however, than merely assigning proper blame for these failed attempts to overrule the market's judgment that this politically powerful industry was not economically viable. Drawing the wrong moral from the S&L affair can have consequences that extend far beyond the boundaries of this ill-fated industry. The American humorist, Mark Twain, once remarked that a cat, having jumped on a hot stove, will never jump on a stove again, even a cold one. Our commercial bank examiners seem to be following precisely this pattern. Commercial banking may not quite be a cold stove at the moment, but it is, at least, a viable industry. Unlike the S&L's, moreover, it plays a critical role in financing businesses, particularly, but not only, those too small or too little known to support direct access to the public security markets. Heavy-handed restrictions on bank loans by examiners misreading the S&L experience will thus raise the cost of capital to, and hence decrease the use of capital by, this important business sector.[7]

---

[7]Examples of such restrictions are the guidelines, recently promulgated jointly by the Federal Deposit Insurance Corporation, the Comptroller of the Currency and the Federal Reserve Board governing so-called Highly Leveraged Transactions (HLT's). These guidelines have effectively shut off lending for corporate restructuring, whether friendly or hostile. But the rules are so vaguely drawn and so uncertain in their application as to be inhibiting other kinds of loans as well. Bank loans these days often carry provisions calling for automatic interest rate increases of 100 basis points or more if the loans are later classified by the bank examiners as HLT's.

Whether regulatory restrictions of these and related kinds have already gone so far as to produce a "credit crunch" of the kind associated in the past with monetary contraction is a subject much being argued at the moment, but one I prefer to leave to the specialists in money and banking. My concerns as a finance specialist are with the longer-run and less directly visible consequences of the current anti-leverage hysteria. This hysteria has already destroyed the liquidity of the market for high-yield bonds. The financial futures markets, currently under heavy attack for their supposed overleveraging, are the next possible candidates for extinction, at least in their U.S. habitats.

Many in academic finance have viewed these ill-founded attacks on our financial markets, particularly the newer markets, with some dismay. But they have, for the most part, stood aside from the controversies. Unlike some of the older fields of economics, the focus in finance has not been on issues of public policy. We have emphasized positive economics rather than normative economics, striving for solid empirical research built on foundations of simple, but powerful organizing theories. Now that our field has officially come of age, as it were, perhaps my colleagues in finance can be persuaded to take their noses out of their data bases from time to time and to bring the insights of our field, and especially the public policy insights, to the attention of a wider audience.

References

Garber, Peter. "Tulipmania." *Journal of Political Economy* 97 (June 1989): 535–560.

Kaplan, Steven N. "The Effects of Management Buyouts on Operations and Value." *Journal of Financial Economics* 24 (June 1989): 217–254.

Miller, Merton H. "Debt and Taxes." *Journal of Finance* 32 (May 1977): 261–275.

———. "The Modigliani–Miller Propositions after Thirty Years." *Journal of Economic Perspectives* 2 (Fall 1988): 99–120.

Modigliani, Franco, and Miller, Merton H. "The Cost of Capital, Corporation Finance and the Theory of Investment." *American Economic Review* 48 (June 1958): 261–297.

———. "Corporate Income Taxes and the Cost of Capital: A Correction." *American Economic Review* 53 (June 1963): 433–443.

The Cost of Capital, Corporation Finance and the Theory of Investment

Franco Modigliani and Merton H. Miller*

What is the "cost of capital" to a firm in a world in which funds are used to acquire assets whose yields are uncertain; and in which capital can be obtained by many different media, ranging from pure debt instruments, representing money-fixed claims, to pure equity issues, giving holders only the right to a pro-rata share in the uncertain venture? This question has vexed at least three classes of economists: (1) the corporation finance specialist concerned with the techniques of financing firms so as to ensure their survival and growth; (2) the managerial economist concerned with capital budgeting; and (3) the economic theorist concerned with explaining investment behavior at both the micro and macro levels.[1]

In much of his formal analysis, the economic theorist at least has tended

*The authors are, respectively, professor and associate professor of economics in the Graduate School of Industrial Administration, Carnegie Institute of Technology. This article is a revised version of a paper delivered at the annual meeting of the Econometric Society, December 1956. The authors express thanks for the comments and suggestions made at that time by the discussants of the paper, Evsey Domar, Robert Eisner and John Lintner, and subsequently by James Duesenberry. They are also greatly indebted to many of their present and former colleagues and students at Carnegie Tech who served so often and with such remarkable patience as a critical forum for the ideas here presented.

[1]The literature bearing on the cost-of-capital problem is far too extensive for listing here. Numerous references to it will be found throughout the paper though we make no claim to completeness. One phase of the problem which we do not consider explicitly, but which has a considerable literature of its own is the relation between the cost of capital and public utility rates. For a recent summary of the "cost-of-capital theory" of rate regulation and a brief discussion of some of its implications, the reader may refer to H. M. Somers [20].

Reprinted from *The American Economic Review*, 48 (June 1958), 261–97, by permission of the authors and the publisher.

to side-step the essence of this cost-of-capital problem by proceeding as though physical assets—like bonds—could be regarded as yielding known, sure streams. Given this assumption, the theorist has concluded that the cost of capital to the owners of a firm is simply the rate of interest on bonds; and has derived the familiar proposition that the firm, acting rationally, will tend to push investment to the point where the marginal yield on physical assets is equal to the market rate of interest.[2] This proposition can be shown to follow from either of two criteria of rational decision-making which are equivalent under certainty, namely (1) the maximization of profits and (2) the maximization of market value.

According to the first criterion, a physical asset is worth acquiring if it will increase the net profit of the owners of the firm. But net profit will increase only if the expected rate of return, or yield, of the asset exceeds the rate of interest. According to the second criterion, an asset is worth acquiring if it increases the value of the owners' equity, *i.e.*, if it adds more to the market value of the firm than the costs of acquisition. But what the asset adds is given by capitalizing the stream it generates at the market rate of interest, and this capitalized value will exceed its cost if and only if the yield of the asset exceeds the rate of interest. Note that, under either formulation, the cost of capital is equal to the rate of interest on bonds, regardless of whether the funds are acquired through debt instruments or through new issues of common stock. Indeed, in a world of sure returns, the distinction between debt and equity funds reduces largely to one of terminology.

It must be acknowledged that some attempt is usually made in this type of analysis to allow for the existence of uncertainty. This attempt typically takes the form of superimposing on the results of the certainty analysis the notion of a "risk discount" to be subtracted from the expected yield (or a "risk premium" to be added to the market rate of interest). Investment decisions are then supposed to be based on a comparison of this "risk adjusted" or "certainty equivalent" yield with the market rate of interest.[3] No satisfactory explanation has yet been provided, however, as to what determines the size of the risk discount and how it varies in response to changes in other variables.

---

[2]Or, more accurately, to the marginal cost of borrowed funds since it is customary, at least in advanced analysis, to draw the supply curve of borrowed funds to the firm as a rising one. For an advanced treatment of the certainty case, see F. and V. Lutz [13].

[3]The classic examples of the certainty-equivalent approach are found in J. R. Hicks [8] and O. Lange [11].

Considered as a convenient approximation, the model of the firm constructed via this certainty—or certainty-equivalent—approach has admittedly been useful in dealing with some of the grosser aspects of the processes of capital accumulation and economic fluctuations. Such a model underlies, for example, the familiar Keynesian aggregate investment function in which aggregate investment is written as a function of the rate of interest—the same riskless rate of interest which appears later in the system in the liquidity-preference equation. Yet few would maintain that this approximation is adequate. At the macroeconomic level there are ample grounds for doubting that the rate of interest has as large and as direct an influence on the rate of investment as this analysis would lead us to believe. At the microeconomic level the certainty model has little descriptive value and provides no real guidance to the finance specialist or managerial economist whose main problems cannot be treated in a framework which deals so cavalierly with uncertainty and ignores all forms of financing other than debt issues. [4]

Only recently have economists begun to face up seriously to the problem of the cost of capital *cum* risk. In the process they have found their interests and endeavors merging with those of the finance specialist and the managerial economist who have lived with the problem longer and more intimately. In this joint search to establish the principles which govern rational investment and financial policy in a world of uncertainty two main lines of attack can be discerned. These lines represent, in effect, attempts to extrapolate to the world of uncertainty each of the two criteria—profit maximization and market value maximization—which were seen to have equivalent implications in the special case of certainty. With the recognition of uncertainty this equivalence vanishes. In fact, the profit maximization criterion is no longer even well defined. Under uncertainty there corresponds to each decision of the firm not a unique profit outcome, but a plurality of mutually exclusive outcomes which can at best be described by a subjective probability distribution. The profit outcome, in short, has become a random variable and as such its maximization no longer has an operational meaning. Nor can this difficulty generally be disposed of by using the mathematical expectation of profits as the variable to be maximized. For decisions which affect the expected value will also tend to affect the dispersion

---

[4]Those who have taken a "case-method" course in finance in recent years will recall in this connection the famous Liquigas case of Hunt and Williams, [9, pp. 193–96] a case which is often used to introduce the student to the cost-of-capital problem and to poke a bit of fun at the economist's certainty-model.

and other characteristics of the distribution of outcomes. In particular, the use of debt rather than equity funds to finance a given venture may well increase the expected return to the owners, but only at the cost of increased dispersion of the outcomes.

Under these conditions the profit outcomes of alternative investment and financing decisions can be compared and ranked only in terms of a *subjective* "utility function" of the owners which weighs the expected yield against other characteristics of the distribution. Accordingly, the extrapolation of the profit maximization criterion of the certainty model has tended to evolve into utility maximization, sometimes explicitly, more frequently in a qualitative and heuristic form. [5]

The utility approach undoubtedly represents an advance over the certainty or certainty-equivalent approach. It does at least permit us to explore (within limits) some of the implications of different financing arrangements, and it does give some meaning to the "cost" of different types of funds. However, because the cost of capital has become an essentially subjective concept, the utility approach has serious drawbacks for normative as well as analytical purposes. How, for example, is management to ascertain the risk preferences of its stockholders and to compromise among their tastes? And how can the economist build a meaningful investment function in the face of the fact that any given investment opportunity might or might not be worth exploiting depending on precisely who happen to be the owners of the firm at the moment?

Fortunately, these questions do not have to be answered; for the alternative approach, based on market value maximization, can provide the basis for an operational definition of the cost of capital and a workable theory of investment. Under this approach any investment project and its concomitant financing plan must pass only the following test: Will the project, as financed, raise the market value of the firm's shares? If so, it is worth undertaking; if not, its return is less than the marginal cost of capital to the firm. Note that such a test is entirely independent of the tastes of the current owners, since market prices will reflect not only their preferences but those of all potential owners as well. If any current stockholder disagrees with management and the market over the valuation of the project, he is free to sell out and reinvest elsewhere,

---

[5]For an attempt at a rigorous explicit development of this line of attack, see F. Modigliani and M. Zeman [14].

but will still benefit from the capital appreciation resulting from management's decision.

The potential advantages of the market-value approach have long been appreciated; yet analytical results have been meager. What appears to be keeping this line of development from achieving its promise is largely the lack of an adequate theory of the effect of financial structure on market valuations, and of how these effects can be inferred from objective market data. It is with the development of such a theory and of its implications for the cost-of-capital problem that we shall be concerned in this paper.

Our procedure will be to develop in Section I the basic theory itself and to give some brief account of its empirical relevance. In Section II, we show how the theory can be used to answer the cost-of-capital question and how it permits us to develop a theory of investment of the firm under conditions of uncertainty. Throughout these sections the approach is essentially a partial-equilibrium one focusing on the firm and "industry." Accordingly, the "prices" of certain income streams will be treated as constant and given from outside the model, just as in the standard Marshallian analysis of the firm and industry the prices of all inputs and of all other products are taken as given. We have chosen to focus at this level rather than on the economy as a whole because it is at the level of the firm and the industry that the interests of the various specialists concerned with the cost-of-capital problem come most closely together. Although the emphasis has thus been placed on partial-equilibrium analysis, the results obtained also provide the essential building blocks for a general equilibrium model which shows how those prices which are here taken as given, are themselves determined. For reasons of space, however, and because the material is of interest in its own right, the presentation of the general equilibrium model which rounds out the analysis must be deferred to a subsequent paper.

I.   The Valuation of Securities, Leverage, and the Cost of Capital

A.   *The Capitalization Rate for Uncertain Streams*

As a starting point, consider an economy in which all physical assets are owned by corporations. For the moment, assume that these corporations can finance their assets by issuing common stock only; the introduction of bond issues, or their equivalent, as a source of corporate funds is postponed until the next part of this section.

The physical assets held by each firm will yield to the owners of the firm—its stockholders—a stream of "profits" over time; but the elements of this series need not be constant and in any event are uncertain. This stream of income, and hence the stream accruing to any share of common stock, will be regarded as extending indefinitely into the future. We assume, however, that the mean value of the stream over time, or average profit per unit of time, is finite and represents a random variable subject to a (subjective) probability distribution. We shall refer to the average value over time of the stream accruing to a given share as the return of that share; and to the mathematical expectation of this average as the expected return of the share. [6] Although individual investors may have different views as to the shape of the probability distribution of the return of any share, we shall assume for simplicity that they are at least in agreement as to the expected return. [7]

This way of characterizing uncertain streams merits brief comment. Notice first that the stream is a stream of profits, not dividends. As will become clear later, as long as management is presumed to be acting in the best interests of the stockholders, retained earnings can be regarded as equivalent to a fully subscribed, pre-emptive issue of common stock. Hence, for present purposes, the division of the stream between cash dividends and retained earnings in any

---

[6]These propositions can be restated analytically as follows: The assets of the ith firm generate a stream:

$$X_i(1), X_i(2) \ldots X_i(T)$$

whose elements are random variables subject to the joint probability distribution:

$$\chi i[X_i(1), X_i(2) \ldots X_i(t)].$$

The return to the ith firm is defined as:

$$X_i = \lim_{T \to \infty} \frac{1}{T} \sum_{t=1}^{T} X_i(t).$$

X_i is itself a random variable with a probability distribution $\phi_i(X_i)$ whose form is determined uniquely by χi. The expected return $\bar{X}_i$ is defined as $\bar{X}_i = E(X_i) = \int x_i X_i \phi_i(X_i) dX_i$. If N_i is the number of shares outstanding, the return of the ith share is $x_i = (1/N)X_i$ with probability distribution $\phi_i(x_i)dx_i = \phi_i(Nx_i)d(Nx_i)$ and expected value $\bar{x}_i = (1/N)\bar{X}_i$.

[7]To deal adequately with refinements such as differences among investors in estimates of expected returns would require extensive discussion of the theory of portfolio selection. Brief references to these and related topics will be made in the succeeding article on the general equilibrium model.

period is a mere detail. Notice also that the uncertainty attaches to the mean value over time of the stream of profits and should not be confused with variability over time of the successive elements of the stream. That variability and uncertainty are two totally different concepts should be clear from the fact that the elements of a stream can be variable even though known with certainty. It can be shown, furthermore, that whether the elements of a stream are sure or uncertain, the effect of variability per se on the valuation of the stream is at best a second-order one which can safely be neglected for our purposes (and indeed most others too).[8]

The next assumption plays a strategic role in the rest of the analysis. We shall assume that firms can be divided into "equivalent return" classes such that the return on the shares issued by any firm in any given class is proportional to (and hence perfectly correlated with) the return on the shares issued by any other firm in the same class. This assumption implies that the various shares within the same class differ, at most, by a "scale factor." Accordingly, if we adjust for the difference in scale, by taking the *ratio* of the return to the expected return, the probability distribution of that ratio is identical for all shares in the class. It follows that all relevant properties of a share are uniquely characterized by specifying (1) the class to which it belongs and (2) its expected return.

The significance of this assumption is that it permits us to classify firms into groups within which the shares of different firms are "homogeneous," that is, perfect substitutes for one another. We have, thus, an analogue to the familiar concept of the industry in which it is the commodity produced by the firms that is taken as homogeneous. To complete this analogy with Marshallian price theory, we shall assume in the analysis to follow that the shares concerned are traded in perfect markets under conditions of atomistic competition.[9]

---

[8]The reader may convince himself of this by asking how much he would be willing to rebate to his employer for the privilege of receiving his annual salary in equal monthly installments rather than in irregular amounts over the year. See also J. M. Keynes [10, esp. pp. 53–54].

[9]Just what our classes of stocks contain and how the different classes can be identified by outside observers are empirical questions to which we shall return later. For the present, it is sufficient to observe: (1) Our concept of a class, while not identical to that of the industry is at least closely related to it. Certainly the basic characteristics of the probability distributions of the returns on assets will depend to a significant extent on the product sold and the technology used. (2) What are the appropriate class boundaries will depend on the particular problem being studied. An economist concerned with general tendencies in the market, for example, might well be prepared to work with far wider classes than would be appropriate for an investor planning his portfolio, or a firm planning its financial strategy.

From our definition of homogeneous classes of stock it follows that in equilibrium in a perfect capital market the price per dollar's worth of expected return must be the same for all shares of any given class. Or, equivalently, in any given class the price of every share must be proportional to its expected return. Let us denote this factor of proportionality for any class, say the kth class, by $1/\rho_k$. Then if p_j denotes the price and $\bar{x}_j$ is the expected return per share of the jth firm in class k, we must have:

$$p_j = \frac{1}{\rho_k} \bar{x}_j; \tag{1}$$

or, equivalently,

$$\frac{\bar{x}_j}{p_j} = \rho_k \quad \text{a constant for all firms } j \text{ in class } k. \tag{2}$$

The constants ρ_k (one for each of the k classes) can be given several economic interpretations: (a) From (2) we see that each ρ_k is the expected rate of return of any share in class k. (b) From (1) $1/\rho_k$ is the price which an investor has to pay for a dollar's worth of expected return in the class k. (c) Again from (1), by analogy with the terminology for perpetual bonds, ρ_k can be regarded as the market rate of capitalization for the expected value of the uncertain streams of the kind generated by the kth class of firms. [10]

B. *Debt Financing and Its Effect on Security Prices*

Having developed an apparatus for dealing with uncertain streams we can now approach the heart of the cost-of-capital problem by dropping the assumption that firms cannot issue bonds. The introduction of debt-financing changes the market for shares in a very fundamental way. Because firms may have different proportions of debt in their capital structure, shares of different companies, even in the same class, can give rise to different probability distributions of returns. In the language of finance, the shares will be subject to different degrees of financial risk or "leverage" and hence they will no longer be perfect substitutes for one another.

---

[10]We cannot, on the basis of the assumptions so far, make any statements about the relationship or spread between the various ρ's or capitalization rates. Before we could do so we would have to make further specific assumptions about the way investors believe the probability distributions vary from class to class, as well as assumptions about investors' preferences as between the characteristics of different distributions.

To exhibit the mechanism determining the relative prices of shares under these conditions, we make the following two assumptions about the nature of bonds and the bond market, though they are actually stronger than is necessary and will be relaxed later: (1) All bonds (including any debts issued by households for the purpose of carrying shares) are assumed to yield a constant income per unit of time, and this income is regarded as certain by all traders regardless of the issuer. (2) Bonds, like stocks, are traded in a perfect market, where the term perfect is to be taken in its usual sense as implying that any two commodities which are perfect substitutes for each other must sell, in equilibrium, at the same price. It follows from assumption (1) that all bonds are in fact perfect substitutes up to a scale factor. It follows from assumption (2) that they must all sell at the same price per dollar's worth of return, or what amounts to the same thing must yield the same rate of return. This rate of return will be denoted by r and referred to as the rate of interest or, equivalently, as the capitalization rate for sure streams. We now can derive the following two basic propositions with respect to the valuation of securities in companies with different capital structures:

Proposition I. Consider any company j and let $\overline{X}_j$ stand as before for the expected return on the assets owned by the company (that is, its expected profit before deduction of interest). Denote by D_j the market value of the debts of the company; by S_j the market value of its common shares; and by $V_j \equiv S_j + D_j$ the market value of all its securities or, as we shall say, the market value of the firm. Then, our Proposition I asserts that we must have in equilibrium:

$$V_j \equiv (S_j + D_j) = \overline{X}_j/\rho_k, \quad \text{for any firm } j \text{ in class } k. \tag{3}$$

That is, the *market value of any firm is independent of its capital structure and is given by capitalizing its expected return at the rate ρ_k appropriate to its class.*

This proposition can be stated in an equivalent way in terms of the firm's "average cost of capital," $\overline{X}_j/V_j$, which is the ratio of its expected return to the market value of all its securities. Our proposition then is:

$$\frac{\overline{X}_j}{(S_j + D_j)} \equiv \frac{\overline{X}_j}{V_j} = \rho_k, \quad \text{for any firm } j, \text{ in class } k. \tag{4}$$

That is, *the average cost of capital to any firm is completely independent of its capital structure and is equal to the capitalization rate of a pure equity stream of its class.*

To establish Proposition I we will show that as long as the relations (3) or (4) do not hold between any pair of firms in a class, arbitrage will take place and restore the stated equalities. We use the term arbitrage advisedly. For if Proposition I did not hold, an investor could buy and sell stocks and bonds in such a way as to exchange one income stream for another stream, identical in all relevant respects but selling at a lower price. The exchange would therefore be advantageous to the investor quite independently of his attitudes toward risk. [11] As investors exploit these arbitrage opportunities, the value of the overpriced shares will fall and that of the underpriced shares will rise, thereby tending to eliminate the discrepancy between the market values of the firms.

By way of proof, consider two firms in the same class and assume for simplicity only, that the expected return, $\overline{X}$, is the same for both firms. Let company 1 be financed entirely with common stock while company 2 has some debt in its capital structure. Suppose first the value of the levered firm, V_2, to be larger than that of the unlevered one, V_1. Consider an investor holding s_2 dollars' worth of the shares of company 2, representing a fraction α of the total outstanding stock, S_2. The return from this portfolio, denoted by Y_2, will be a fraction α of the income available for the stockholders of company 2, which is equal to the total return X_2 less the interest charge, rD_2. Since under our assumption of homogeneity, the anticipated total return of company 2, X_2, is, under all circumstances, the same as the anticipated total return to company 1, X_1, we can hereafter replace X_2 and X_1 by a common symbol X. Hence, the return from the initial portfolio can be written as:

$$Y_2 = \alpha(X - rD_2). \tag{5}$$

Now suppose the investor sold his αS_2 worth of company 2 shares and acquired instead an amount $s_1 = \alpha(S_2 + D_2)$ of the shares of company 1. He could do so by utilizing the amount αS_2 realized from the sale of his initial holding and borrowing an additional amount αD_2 on his own credit, pledging his new holdings in company 1 as a collateral. He would thus secure for himself a fraction $s_1/S_1 = \alpha(S_2 + D_2)/S_1$ of the shares and earnings of company 1. Making

---

[11] In the language of the theory of choice, the exchanges are movements from inefficient points in the interior to efficient points on the boundary of the investor's opportunity set; and not movements between efficient points along the boundary. Hence for this part of the analysis nothing is involved in the way of specific assumptions about investor attitudes or behavior other than that investors behave consistently and prefer more income to less income, *ceteris paribus*.

proper allowance for the interest payments on his personal debt αD_2, the return from the new portfolio, Y_1, is given by:

$$Y_1 = \frac{\alpha(S_2 + D_2)}{S_1}X - r\alpha D_2 = \alpha\frac{V_2}{V_1}X - r\alpha D_2. \tag{6}$$

Comparing (5) with (6) we see that as long as $V_2 > V_1$ we must have $Y_1 > Y_2$, so that it pays owners of company 2's shares to sell their holdings, thereby depressing S_2 and hence V_2; and to acquire shares of company 1, thereby raising S_1 and thus V_1. We conclude therefore that levered companies cannot command a premium over unlevered companies because investors have the opportunity of putting the equivalent leverage into their portfolio directly by borrowing on personal account.

Consider now the other possibility, namely that the market value of the levered company V_2 is less than V_1. Suppose an investor holds initially an amount s_1 of shares of company 1, representing a fraction α of the total out-standing stock, S_1. His return from this holding is:

$$Y_1 = \frac{s_1}{S_1}X = \alpha X.$$

Suppose he were to exchange this initial holding for another portfolio, also worth s_1, but consisting of s_2 dollars of stock of company 2 and of d dollars of bonds, where s_2 and d are given by:

$$s_2 = \frac{S_2}{V_2}s_1, \quad d = \frac{D_2}{V_2}s_1. \tag{7}$$

In other words the new portfolio is to consist of stock of company 2 and of bonds in the proportions S_2/V_2 and D_2/V_2, respectively. The return from the stock in the new portfolio will be a fraction s_2/S_2 of the total return to stockholders of company 2, which is $(X - rD_2)$, and the return from the bonds will be rd. Making use of (7), the total return from the portfolio, Y_2, can be expressed as follows:

$$Y_2 = \frac{s_2}{S_2}(X - rD_2) + rd = \frac{s_1}{V_2}(X - rD_2) + r\frac{D_2}{V_2}s_1 = \frac{s_1}{V_2}X = \alpha\frac{S_1}{V_2}X$$

(since $s_1 = \alpha S_1$). Comparing Y_2 with Y_1 we see that, if $V_2 < S_1 \equiv V_1$, then Y_2 will exceed Y_1. Hence it pays the holders of company 1's shares to sell these holdings and replace them with a mixed portfolio containing an appropriate fraction of the shares of company 2.

The acquisition of a mixed portfolio of stock of a levered company j and of bonds in the proportion S_j/V_j and D_j/V_j respectively, may be regarded as an operation which "undoes" the leverage, giving access to an appropriate fraction of the unlevered return X_j. It is this possibility of undoing leverage which prevents the value of levered firms from being consistently less than those of unlevered firms, or more generally prevents the average cost of capital $\overline{X}_j/V_j$ from being systematically higher for levered than for nonlevered companies in the same class. Since we have already shown that arbitrage will also prevent V_2 from being larger than V_1, we can conclude that in equilibrium we must have $V_2 = V_1$, as stated in Proposition I.

Proposition II. From Proposition I we can derive the following proposition concerning the rate of return on common stock in companies whose capital structure includes some debt: the expected rate of return or yield, i, on the stock of any company j belonging to the kth class is a linear function of leverage as follows:

$$i_j = \rho_k + (\rho_k - r)D_j/S_j. \tag{8}$$

That is, *the expected yield of a share of stock is equal to the appropriate capitalization rate ρ_k for a pure equity stream in the class, plus a premium related to financial risk equal to the debt-to-equity ratio times the spread between ρ_k and r.* Or equivalently, the market price of any share of stock is given by capitalizing its expected return at the continuously variable rate i_j of (8). [12]

A number of writers have stated close equivalents of our Proposition I although by appealing to intuition rather than by attempting a proof and only to insist immediately that the results were not applicable to the actual capital markets. [13] Proposition II, however, so far as we have been able to discover is

---

[12]To illustrate, suppose $\overline{X} = 1000$, $D = 4000$, $r = 5$ per cent and $\rho_k = 10$ per cent. These values imply $V = 10{,}000$ and $S = 6000$ by virtue of Proposition I. The expected yield or rate of return per share is then:

$$i = \frac{1000 - 200}{6000} = .1 + (.1 - .05)\frac{4000}{6000} = 13\tfrac{1}{3} \text{ per cent.}$$

[13]See, for example, J. B. Williams [21, esp. pp. 72–73]; David Durand [3]; and W. A. Morton [15]. None of these writers describe in any detail the mechanism which is supposed to keep the average cost of capital constant under changes in capital structure. They seem, however, to be visualizing the equilibrating mechanism in terms of switches by investors between stocks and bonds as the yields of each get out of line

new.[14] To establish it we first note that, by definition, the expected rate of return, i, is given by:

$$i_j = \frac{\overline{X}_j - rD_j}{S_j}.$$ (9)

From Proposition I, equation (3), we know that:

$$\overline{X}_j = \rho_k(S_j + D_j).$$

Substituting in (9) and simplifying, we obtain equation (8).

C. *Some Qualifications and Extensions of the Basic Propositions*

The methods and results developed so far can be extended in a number of useful directions, of which we shall consider here only three: (1) allowing for a corporate profits tax under which interest payments are deductible; (2) recognizing the existence of a multiplicity of bonds and interest rates; and (3) acknowledging the presence of market imperfections which might interfere with the process of arbitrage. The first two will be examined briefly in this section with some further attention given to the tax problem in Section II. Market imperfections will be discussed in Part D of this section in the course of a comparison of our results with those of received doctrines in the field of finance.

Effects of the Present Method of Taxing Corporations. The deduction of interest in computing taxable corporate profits will prevent the arbitrage process from making the value of all firms in a given class proportional to the expected returns generated by their physical assets. Instead, it can be shown (by the same type of proof used for the original version of Proposition I) that the market values of firms in each class must be proportional in equilibrium to their expected return net of taxes (that is, to the sum of the interest paid and expected net stockholder income). This means we must replace each $\overline{X}_j$ in the original versions of Propositions I and II with new variable $\overline{X}_j^{\tau}$ representing the total income net of taxes generated by the firm:

$$\overline{X}_j^{\tau} \equiv (\overline{X}_j - rD_j)(1 - \tau) + rD_j \equiv \overline{\pi}_j^{\tau} + rD_j,$$ (10)

---

with their "riskiness." This is an argument quite different from the pure arbitrage mechanism underlying our proof, and the difference is crucial. Regarding Proposition I as resting on investors' attitudes toward risk leads inevitably to a misunderstanding of many factors influencing relative yields such as, for example, limitations on the portfolio composition of financial institutions. See below, esp. Section I.D.

[14]Morton does make reference to a linear yield function but only ". . . for the sake of simplicity and because the particular function used makes no essential difference in my conclusions" [15, p. 443, note 2].

where $\overline{\pi}_j^\tau$ represents the expected net income accruing to the common stockholders and τ stands for the average rate of corporate income tax. [15]

After making these substitutions, the propositions, when adjusted for taxes, continue to have the same form as their originals. That is, Proposition I becomes:

$$\frac{\overline{X}_j^\tau}{V_j} = \rho_k^\tau, \quad \text{for any firm in class } k, \tag{11}$$

and Proposition II becomes

$$i_j \equiv \frac{\overline{\pi}_j^\tau}{S_j} = \rho_j^\tau + (\rho_k^\tau - r)D_j/S_j \tag{12}$$

where ρ_k^τ is the capitalization rate for income net of taxes in class k.

Although the form of the propositions is unaffected, certain interpretations must be changed. In particular, the after-tax capitalization rate ρ_k^τ can no longer be identified with the "average cost of capital" which is $\rho_k = \overline{X}_j/V_j$. The difference between ρ_k^τ and the "true" average cost of capital, as we shall see, is a matter of some relevance in connection with investment planning within the firm (Section II). For the description of market behavior, however, which is our immediate concern here, the distinction is not essential. To simplify presentation, therefore, and to preserve continuity with the terminology in the standard literature we shall continue in this section to refer to ρ_k^τ as the average cost of capital, though strictly speaking this identification is correct only in the absence of taxes.

Effects of a Plurality of Bonds and Interest Rates. In existing capital markets we find not one, but a whole family of interest rates varying with maturity, with the technical provisions of the loan and, what is most relevant for present purposes, with the financial condition of the borrower. [16] Economic theory and market experience both suggest that the yields demanded by lenders tend to increase with the debt–equity ratio of the borrowing firm (or

---

[15]For simplicity, we shall ignore throughout the tiny element of progression in our present corporate tax and treat τ as a constant independent of $(X_j - rD_j)$.

[16]We shall not consider here the extension of the analysis to encompass the time structure of interest rates. Although some of the problems posed by the time structure can be handled within our comparative statics framework, an adequate discussion would require a separate paper.

individual). If so, and if we can assume as a first approximation that this yield curve, $r = r(D/S)$, whatever its precise form, is the same for all borrowers, then we can readily extend our propositions to the case of a rising supply curve for borrowed funds. [17]

Proposition I is actually unaffected in form and interpretation by the fact that the rate of interest may rise with leverage; while the average cost of *borrowed* funds will tend to increase as debt rises, the average cost of funds from *all* sources will still be independent of leverage (apart from the tax effect). This conclusion follows directly from the ability of those who engage in arbitrage to undo the leverage in any financial structure by acquiring an appropriately mixed portfolio of bonds and stocks. Because of this ability, the ratio of earnings (*before* interest charges) to market value—*i.e.*, the average cost of capital from all sources—must be the same for all firms in a given class. [18] In other words, the increased cost of borrowed funds as leverage increases will tend to be offset by a corresponding reduction in the yield of common stock. This seemingly paradoxical result will be examined more closely below in connection with Proposition II.

A significant modification of Proposition I would be required only if the yield curve $r = r(D/S)$ were different for different borrowers, as might happen if creditors had marked preferences for the securities of a particular class of

---

[17] We can also develop a theory of bond valuation along lines essentially parallel to those followed for the case of shares. We conjecture that the curve of bond yields as a function of leverage will turn out to be a nonlinear one in contrast to the linear function of leverage developed for common shares. However, we would also expect that the rate of increase in the yield on new issues would not be substantial in practice. This relatively slow rise would reflect the fact that interest rate increases by themselves can never be completely satisfactory to creditors as compensation for their increased risk. Such increase may simply serve to raise r so high relative to ρ that they become self-defeating by giving rise to a situation in which even normal fluctuations in earnings may force the company into bankruptcy. The difficulty of borrowing more, therefore, tends to show up in the usual case not so much in higher rates as in the form of increasingly stringent restrictions imposed on the company's management and finances by the creditors; and ultimately in a complete inability to obtain new borrowed funds, at least from the institutional investors who normally set the standards in the market for bonds.

[18] One normally minor qualification might be noted. Once we relax the assumption that all bonds have certain yields, our arbitrage operator faces the danger of something comparable to "gambler's ruin." That is, there is always the possibility that an otherwise sound concern—one whose long-run expected income is greater than its interest liability—might be forced into liquidation as a result of a run of temporary losses. Since reorganization generally involves costs, and because the operation of the firm may be hampered during the period of reorganization with lasting unfavorable effects on earnings prospects, we might perhaps expect heavily levered companies to sell at a slight discount relative to less heavily indebted companies of the same class.

debtors. If, for example, corporations as a class were able to borrow at lower rates than individuals having equivalent personal leverage, then the average cost of capital to corporations might fall slightly, as leverage increased over some range, in reflection of this differential. In evaluating this possibility, however, remember that the relevant interest rate for our arbitrage operators is the rate on brokers' loans and, historically, that rate has not been noticeably higher than representative corporate rates. [19] The operations of holding companies and investment trusts which can borrow on terms comparable to operating companies represent still another force which could be expected to wipe out any marked or prolonged advantages from holding levered stocks. [20]

Although Proposition I remains unaffected as long as the yield curve is the same for all borrowers, the relation between common stock yields and leverage will no longer be the strictly linear one given by the original Proposition II. If r increases with leverage, the yield i will still tend to rise as D/S increases, but at a decreasing rather than a constant rate. Beyond some high level of leverage, depending on the exact form of the interest function, the yield may even start to fall. [21] The relation between i and D/S could conceivably take the form indicated by the curve MD in Figure 2, although in practice the curvature would be much less pronounced. By contrast, with a constant rate of interest, the relation would be linear throughout as shown by line MM', Figure 2.

The downward sloping part of the curve MD perhaps requires some comment since it may be hard to imagine why investors, other than those who

---

[19] Under normal conditions, moreover, a substantial part of the arbitrage process could be expected to take the form, not of having the arbitrage operators go into debt on personal account to put the required leverage into their portfolios, but simply of having them reduce the amount of corporate bonds they already hold when they acquire underpriced unlevered stock. Margin requirements are also somewhat less of an obstacle to maintaining any desired degree of leverage in a portfolio than might be thought at first glance. Leverage could be largely restored in the face of higher margin requirements by switching to stocks having more leverage at the corporate level.

[20] An extreme form of inequality between borrowing and lending rates occurs, of course, in the case of preferred stocks, which can not be directly issued by individuals on personal account. Here again, however, we would expect that the operations of investment corporations plus the ability of arbitrage operators to sell off their holdings of preferred stocks would act to prevent the emergence of any substantial premiums (for this reason) on capital structures containing preferred stocks. Nor are preferred stocks so far removed from bonds as to make it impossible for arbitrage operators to approximate closely the risk and leverage of a corporate preferred stock by incurring a somewhat smaller debt on personal account.

[21] Since new lenders are unlikely to permit this much leverage (cf. note 17), this range of the curve is likely to be occupied by companies whose earnings prospects have fallen substantially since the time when their debts were issued.

like lotteries, would purchase stocks in this range. Remember, however, that the yield curve of Proposition II is a consequence of the more fundamental Proposition I. Should the demand by the risk-lovers prove insufficient to keep the market to the peculiar yield-curve *MD*, this demand would be reinforced by the action of arbitrage operators. The latter would find it profitable to own a pro-rata share of the firm as a whole by holding its stock *and* bonds, the lower yield of the shares being thus offset by the higher return on bonds.

D.   *The Relation of Propositions I and II to Current Doctrines*

The propositions we have developed with respect to the valuation of firms and shares appear to be substantially at variance with current doctrines in the field of finance. The main differences between our view and the current view are summarized graphically in Figures 1 and 2. Our Proposition I [equation (4)] asserts that the average cost of capital, $\overline{X}_j^\tau/V_j$, is a constant for all firms j in class k, independently of their financial structure. This implies that, if we were to take a sample of firms in a given class, and if for each firm we were to plot the ratio of expected return to market value against some measure of leverage or financial structure, the points would tend to fall on a horizontal straight line with intercept ρ_k^τ like the sold line *mm'* in Figure 1. [22] From Proposition I we derived Proposition II [equation (8)] which, taking the simplest version with r constant, asserts that, for all firms in a class, the relation between the yield on common stock and financial structure, measured by D_j/S_j, will approximate a straight line with slope $(\rho_k^\tau - r)$ and intercept ρ_k^τ. This relationship is shown as the solid line *MM'* in Figure 2, to which reference has been made earlier. [23]

By contrast, the conventional view among finance specialists appears to start from the proposition that, other things equal, the earnings–price ratio (or its reciprocal, the times–earning multiplier) of a firm's common stock will normally be only slightly affected by "moderate" amounts of debt in the firm's

---

[22] In Figure 1 the measure of leverage used is D_j/V_j (the ratio of debt to market value) rather than D_j/S_j (the ratio of debt to equity), the concept used in the analytical development. The D_j/V_j measure is introduced at this point because it simplifies comparison and contrast of our view with the traditional position.

[23] The line *MM'* in Figure 2 has been drawn with a positive slope on the assumption that $\rho_k^\tau > r$, a condition which will normally obtain. Our Proposition II as given in equation (8) would continue to be valid, of course, even in the unlikely event that $\rho_k^\tau < r$, but the slope of *MM'* would be negative.

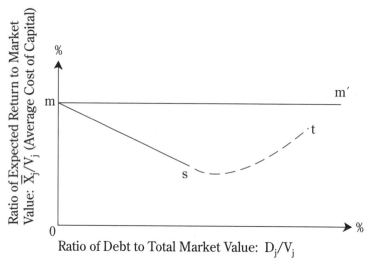

Figure 1

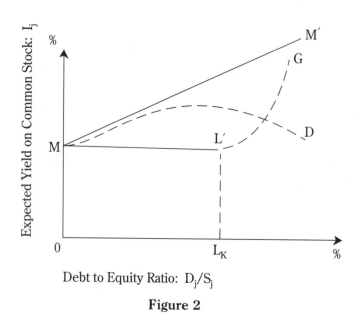

Figure 2

capital structure.[24] Translated into our notation, it asserts that for any firm j in the class k,

$$\frac{\overline{X}_j^\tau - rD_j}{S_j} \equiv \frac{\overline{\pi}_j^\tau}{S_j} = i_k^*, \quad \text{a constant for } \frac{D_j}{S_j} \leq L_k \tag{13}$$

or, equivalently,

$$S_j = \overline{\pi}_j^\tau / i_k^*. \tag{14}$$

Here i_k^* represents the capitalization rate or earnings–price ratio on the common stock and L_k denotes some amount of leverage regarded as the maximum "reasonable" amount for firms of the class k. This assumed relationship between yield and leverage is the horizontal solid line ML' of Figure 2. Beyond L', the yield will presumably rise sharply as the market discounts "excessive" trading on the equity. This possibility of a rising range for high leverages is indicated by the broken-line segment $L'G$ in the figure.[25]

If the value of shares were really given by (14) then the over-all market value of the firm must be:

$$V_j \equiv S_j + D_j = \frac{\overline{X}_j^\tau - rD_j}{i_k^*} + D_j = \frac{\overline{X}_j^\tau}{i_k^*} + \frac{(i_k^* - r)D_j}{i_k^*}. \tag{16}$$

That is, for any given level of expected total returns after taxes $(\overline{X}_j^\tau)$ and assuming, as seems natural, that $i_k^* > r$, the value of the firm must tend to *rise* with debt;[26] whereas our Proposition I asserts that the value of the firm is completely independent of the capital structure. Another way of contrasting our

---

[24]See, *e.g.*, Graham and Dodd [6, pp. 464–66]. Without doing violence to this position, we can bring out its implications more sharply by ignoring the qualification and treating the yield as a virtual constant over the relevant range. See in this connection the discussion in Durand [3, esp. pp. 225–37] of what he calls the "net income method" of valuation.

[25]To make it easier to see some of the implications of this hypothesis as well as to prepare the ground for later statistical testing, it will be helpful to assume that the notion of a critical limit on leverage beyond which yields rise rapidly, can be epitomized by a quadratic relation of the form:

$$\overline{\pi}_j^\tau / S_j = i_k^* + \beta(D_j/S_j) + \alpha(D_j/S_j)^2, \quad \alpha > 0. \tag{15}$$

[26]For a typical discussion of how a promoter can, supposedly, increase the market value of a firm by recourse to debt issues, see W. J. Eiteman [4, esp. pp. 11–13].

position with the traditional one is in terms of the cost of capital. Solving (16) for $\overline{X}_j^\tau/V_j$ yields:

$$\overline{X}_j^\tau/V_j = i_k^* - (i_k^* - r)D_j/V_j. \tag{17}$$

According to this equation, the average cost of capital is not independent of capital structure as we have argued, but should tend to *fall* with increasing leverage, at least within the relevant range of moderate debt ratios, as shown by the line *ms* in Figure 1. Or to put it in more familiar terms, debt-financing should be "cheaper" than equity-financing if not carried too far.

When we also allow for the possibility of a rising range of stock yields for large values of leverage, we obtain a U-shaped curve like *mst* in Figure 1.[27] That a yield-curve for stocks of the form *ML'G* in Figure 2 implies a U-shaped cost-of-capital curve has, of course, been recognized by many writers. A natural further step has been to suggest that the capital structure corresponding to the trough of the U is an "optimal capital structure" towards which management ought to strive in the best interests of the stockholders.[28] According to our model, by contrast, no such optimal structure exists—all structures being equivalent from the point of view of the cost of capital.

Although the falling, or at least U-shaped, cost-of-capital function is in one form or another the dominant view in the literature, the ultimate rationale of that view is by no means clear. The crucial element in the position—that the expected earnings–price ratio of the stock is largely unaffected by leverage up to some conventional limit—is rarely even regarded as something which requires explanation. It is usually simply taken for granted or it is merely

---

[27]The U-shaped nature of the cost-of-capital curve can be exhibited explicitly if the yield curve for shares as a function of leverage can be approximated by equation (15) of footnote 25. From that equation, multiplying both sides by S_j we obtain: $\pi_j^\tau = \overline{X}_j^\tau - rD_j = i_k^* S_j + \beta D_j + \alpha D_j^2/S_j$ or, adding and subtracting $i_k^* D_k$ from the right-hand side and collecting terms,

$$\overline{X}_j^\tau = i_k^*(S_j + D_j) + (\beta + r - i_k^*)D_j + \alpha D_j^2/S_j. \tag{18}$$

Dividing (18) by V_j gives an expression for the cost of capital:

$$\overline{X}_j^\tau/V_j = i_k^* - (i_k^* - r - \beta)D_j/V_j + \alpha D_j^2/S_jV_j = i_k^* - (i_k^* - r - \beta)D_j/V_j + \alpha(D_j/V_j)^2/(1 - D_j/V_j) \tag{19}$$

which is clearly U-shaped since α is supposed to be positive.

[28]For a typical statement see S. M. Robbins [16, p. 307]. See also Graham and Dodd [6, pp. 468–74].

asserted that this is the way the market behaves.[29] To the extent that the constant earnings–price ratio has a rationale at all we suspect that it reflects in most cases the feeling that moderate amounts of debt in "sound" corporations do not really add very much to the "riskiness" of the stock. Since the extra risk is slight, it seems natural to suppose that firms will not have to pay noticeably higher yields in order to induce investors to hold the stock.[30]

A more sophisticated line of argument has been advanced by David Durand [3, pp. 231–33]. He suggests that because insurance companies and certain other important institutional investors are restricted to debt securities, nonfinancial corporations are able to borrow from them at interest rates which are lower than would be required to compensate creditors in a free market. Thus, while he would presumably agree with our conclusions that stockholders could not gain from leverage in an unconstrained market, he concludes that they can gain under present institutional arrangements. This gain would arise by virtue of the "safety superpremium" which lenders are willing to pay corporations for the privilege of lending.[31]

The defective link in both the traditional and the Durand version of the argument lies in the confusion between investors' subjective risk preferences and their objective market opportunities. Our Propositions I and II, as noted earlier, do not depend for their validity on any assumption about individual risk preferences. Nor do they involve any assertion as to what is an adequate compensation to investors for assuming a given degree of risk. They rely merely on the fact that a given commodity cannot consistently sell at more than one price in the market; or more precisely that the price of a commodity

---

[29]See *e.g.*, Graham and Dodd [6, p. 466].

[30]A typical statement is the following by Guthmann and Dougall [7, p. 245]: "Theoretically it might be argued that the increased hazard from using bonds and preferred stocks would counterbalance this additional income and so prevent the common stock from being more attractive than when it had a lower return but fewer prior obligations. In practice, the extra earnings from 'trading on the equity' are often regarded by investors as more than sufficient to serve as a 'premium for risk' when the proportions of the several securities are judiciously mixed."

[31]Like Durand, Morton [15] contends "that the actual market deviates from [Proposition I] by giving a changing over-all cost of money at different points of the [leverage] scale" (p. 443, note 2, inserts ours), but the basis for this contention is nowhere clearly stated. Judging by the great emphasis given to the lack of mobility of investment funds between stocks and bonds and to the psychological and institutional pressures toward debt portfolios (see pp. 444–51 and especially his discussion of the optimal capital structure on p. 453) he would seem to be taking a position very similar to that of Durand above.

127

representing a "bundle" of two other commodities cannot be consistently different from the weighted average of the prices of the two components (the weights being equal to the proportion of the two commodities in the bundle).

An analogy may be helpful at this point. The relations between $1/\rho_k$, the price per dollar of an unlevered stream in class k; $1/r$, the price per dollar of a sure stream, and $1/i_j$, the price per dollar of a levered stream j, in the kth class, are essentially the same as those between, respectively, the price of whole milk, the price of butter fat, and the price of milk which has been thinned out by skimming off some of the butter fat. Our Proposition I states that a firm cannot reduce the cost of capital—*i.e.*, increase the market value of the stream it generates—by securing part of its capital through the sale of bonds, even though debt money appears to be cheaper. This assertion is equivalent to the proposition that, under perfect markets, a dairy farmer cannot in general earn more for the milk he produces by skimming some of the butter fat and selling it separately, even though butter fat per unit weight, sells for more than whole milk. The advantage from skimming the milk rather than selling whole milk would be purely illusory; for what would be gained from selling the high-priced butter fat would be lost in selling the low-priced residue of thinned milk. Similarly our Proposition II—that the price per dollar of a levered stream falls as leverage increases—is an exact analogue of the statement that the price per gallon of thinned milk falls continuously as more butter fat is skimmed off. [32]

---

[32] Let M denote the quantity of whole milk, B/M the proportion of butter fat in the whole milk, and let p_M, p_B and p_α denote, respectively, the price per unit weight of whole milk, butter fat and thinned milk from which a fraction α of the butter fat has been skimmed off. We then have the fundamental perfect market relation:

$$p_\alpha(M - \alpha B) + p_B \alpha B = p_M M, \quad 0 \leq \alpha \leq 1, \tag{a}$$

stating that total receipts will be the same amount $p_M M$, independently of the amount αB of butter fat that may have been sold separately. Since p_M corresponds to $1/\rho$, p_B to $1/r$, p_α to $1/i$, M to $\overline{X}$ and αB to rD, (a) is equivalent to Proposition I, $S + D = \overline{X}/\rho$. From (a) we derive:

$$p_\alpha = p_M \frac{M}{M - \alpha B} - p_B \frac{\alpha B}{M - \alpha B} \tag{b}$$

which gives the price of thinned milk as an explicit function of the proportion of butter fat skimmed off; the function decreasing as long as $p_B > p_M$. From (a) also follows:

$$1/p_\alpha = 1/p_M + (1/p_M - 1/p_B) \frac{p_B \alpha B}{p_\alpha(M - \alpha B)} \tag{c}$$

which is the exact analogue of Proposition II, as given by (8).

It is clear that this last assertion is true as long as butter fat is worth more per unit weight than whole milk, and it holds even if, for many consumers, taking a little cream out of the milk (adding a little leverage to the stock) does not detract noticeably from the taste (does not add noticeably to the risk). Furthermore the argument remains valid even in the face of instituional [*sic*] limitations of the type envisaged by Durand. For suppose that a large fraction of the population habitually dines in restaurants which are required by law to serve only cream in lieu of milk (entrust their savings to institutional investors who can only buy bonds). To be sure the price of butter fat will then tend to be higher in relation to that of skimmed milk than in the absence [of] such restrictions (the rate of interest will tend to be lower), and this will benefit people who eat at home and who like skim milk (who manage their own portfolio and are able and willing to take risk). But it will still be the case that a farmer cannot gain by skimming some of the butter fat and selling it separately (firm cannot reduce the cost of capital by recourse to borrowed funds.)[33]

Our propositions can be regarded as the extension of the classical theory of markets to the particular case of the capital markets. Those who hold the current view—whether they realize it or not—must assume not merely that there are lags and frictions in the equilibrating process—a feeling we certainly share,[34] claiming for our propositions only that they describe the central tendency around which observations will scatter—but also that there are large and *systematic* imperfections in the market which permanently bias the outcome. This is an assumption that economists, at any rate, will instinctively eye with some skepticism.

In any event, whether such prolonged, systematic departures from equilibrium really exist or whether our propositions are better descriptions of long-run market behavior can be settled only by empirical research. Before

---

[33]The reader who likes parables will find that the analogy with interrelated commodity markets can be pushed a good deal farther than we have done in the text. For instance, the effect of changes in the market rate of interest on the over-all cost of capital is the same as the effect of a change in the price of butter on the price of whole milk. Similarly, just as the relation between the prices of skim milk and butter fat influences the kind of cows that will be reared, so the relation between i and r influences the kind of ventures that will be undertaken. If people like butter we shall have Guernseys; if they are willing to pay a high price for safety, this will encourage ventures which promise smaller but less uncertain streams per dollar of physical assets.

[34]Several specific examples of the failure of the arbitrage mechanism can be found in Graham and Dodd [6, *e.g.*, pp. 646–48]. The price discrepancy described on pp. 646–47 is particularly curious since it persists even today despite the fact that a whole generation of security analysts has been brought up on this book!

going on to the theory of investment it may be helpful, therefore, to look at the evidence.

E. Some Preliminary Evidence on the Basic Propositions

Unfortunately the evidence which has been assembled so far is amazingly skimpy. Indeed, we have been able to locate only two recent studies—and these of rather limited scope—which were designed to throw light on the issue. Pending the results of more comprehensive tests which we hope will soon be available, we shall review briefly such evidence as is provided by the two studies in question: (1) an analysis of the relation between security yields and financial structure for some 43 large electric utilities by F. B. Allen [1], and (2) a parallel (unpublished) study by Robert Smith [19], for 42 oil companies designed to test whether Allen's rather striking results would be found in an industry with very different characteristics. [35] The Allen study is based on average figures for the years 1947 and 1948, while the Smith study relates to the single year 1953.

The Effect of Leverage on the Cost of Capital. According to the received view, as shown in equation (17) the average cost of capital $\overline{X}^\tau/V$, should decline linearly with leverage as measured by the ratio D/V, at least through most of the relevant range. [36] According to Proposition I, the average cost of capital within a given class k should tend to have the same value ρ_k^τ independently of the degree of leverage. A simple test of the merits of the two alternative hypotheses can thus be carried out by correlating $\overline{X}^\tau/V$ with D/V. If the traditional view is correct, the correlation should be significantly negative; if our view represents a better approximation to reality, then the correlation should not be significantly different from zero.

Both studies provide information about the average value of D—the market value of bonds and preferred stock—and of V—the market value of all

---

[35] We wish to express our thanks to both writers for making available to us some of their original worksheets. In addition to these recent studies there is a frequently cited (but apparently seldom read) study by the Federal Communications Commission in 1938 [22] which purports to show the existence of an optimal capital structure or range of structures (in the sense defined above) for public utilities in the 1930's. By current standards for statistical investigations, however, this study cannot be regarded as having any real evidential value for the problem at hand.

[36] We shall simplify our notation in this section by dropping the subscript j used to denote a particular firm wherever this will not lead to confusion.

securities. [37] From these data we can readily compute the ratio D/V and this ratio (expressed as a percentage) is represented by the symbol d in the regression equations below. The measurement of the variable $\overline{X}^\tau/V$, however, presents serious difficulties. Strictly speaking, the numerator should measure the expected returns net of taxes, but this is a variable on which no direct information is available. As an approximation, we have followed both authors and used (1) the average value of actual net returns in 1947 and 1948 for Allen's utilities; and (2) actual net returns in 1953 for Smith's oil companies. Net return is defined in both cases as the sum of interest, preferred dividends and stockholders' income net of corporate income taxes. Although this approximation to expected returns is undoubtedly very crude, there is no reason to believe that it will systematically bias the test in so far as the sign of the regression coefficient is concerned. The roughness of the approximation, however, will tend to make for a wide scatter. Also contributing to the scatter is the crudeness of the industrial classification, since especially within the sample of oil companies, the assumption that all the firms belong to the same class in our sense, is at best only approximately valid.

Denoting by x our approximation to $\overline{X}^\tau/V$ (expressed, like d, as a percentage), the results of the tests are as follows:

Electric Utilities $\quad x = 5.3 + .006d \quad r = .12$
$$(\pm\ .008)$$

Oil Companies $\quad x = 8.5 + .006d \quad r = .04.$
$$(\pm\ .024)$$

The data underlying these equations are also shown in scatter diagram form in Figures 3 and 4.

The results of these tests are clearly favorable to our hypothesis. Both correlation coefficients are very close to zero and not statistically significant.

---

[37]Note that for purposes of this test preferred stocks, since they represent an *expected* fixed obligation, are properly classified with bonds even though the tax status of preferred dividends is different from that of interest payments and even though preferred dividends are really fixed only as to their maximum in any year. Some difficulty of classification does arise in the case of convertible preferred stocks (and convertible bonds) selling at a substantial premium, but fortunately very few such issues were involved for the companies included in the two studies. Smith included bank loans and certain other short-term obligations (at book values) in his data on oil company debts and this treatment is perhaps open to some question. However, the amounts involved were relatively small and check computations showed that their elimination would lead to only minor differences in the test results.

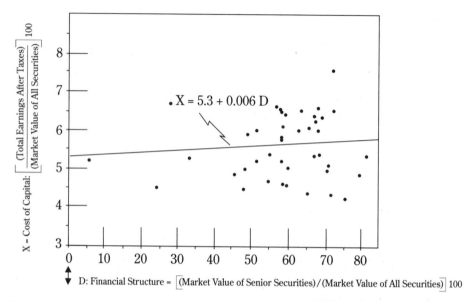

Figure 3   Cost of Capital in Relation to Financial Structure for 43 Electric Utilities, 1947–48

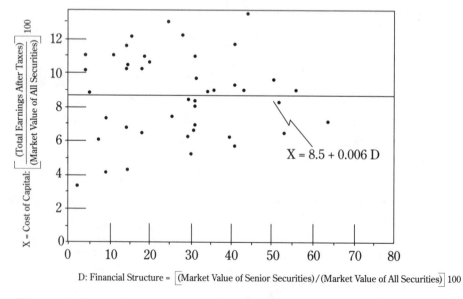

Figure 4   Cost of Capital in Relation to Financial Structure for 42 Oil Companies, 1953

Furthermore, the implications of the traditional view fail to be supported even with respect to the sign of the correlation. The data in short provide no evidence of any tendency for the cost of capital to fall as the debt ratio increases. [38]

It should also be apparent from the scatter diagrams that there is no hint of a curvilinear, U-shaped, relation of the kind which is widely believed to hold between the cost of capital leverage. This graphical impression was confirmed by statistical tests which showed that for both industries the curvature was not significantly different from zero, its sign actually being opposite to that hypothesized. [39]

Note also that according to our model, the constant terms of the regression equations are measures of ρ_k^τ, the capitalization rates for unlevered streams and hence the average cost of capital in the classes in question. The estimates of 8.5 per cent for the oil companies as against 5.3 per cent for electric utilities appear to accord well with a priori expectations, both in absolute value and relative spread.

The Effect of Leverage on Common Stock Yields. According to our Proposition II—see equation 12 and Figure 2—the expected yield on common

---

[38]It may be argued that a test of the kind used is biased against the traditional view. The fact that both sides of the regression equation are divided by the variable V which may be subject to random variation might tend to impart a positive bias to the correlation. As a check on the results presented in the text, we have, therefore, carried out a supplementary test based on equation (16). This equation shows that, if the traditional view is correct, the market value of a company should, for given $\overline{X}^\tau$, increase with debt through most of the relevant range; according to our model the market value should be uncorrelated with D, given $\overline{X}^\tau$. Because of wide variations in the size of the firms included in our samples, all variables must be divided by a suitable scale factor in order to avoid spurious results in carrying out a test of equation (16). The factor we have used is the book value of the firm denoted by A. The hypothesis tested thus takes the specific form:

$$V/A = a + b(\overline{X}^\tau/A) + c(D/A)$$

and the numerator of the ratio X^τ/A is again approximated by actual net returns. The partial correlation between V/A and D/A should now be positive according to the traditional view and zero according to our model. Although division by A should, if anything, bias the results in favor of the traditional hypothesis, the partial correlation turns out to be only .03 for the oil companies and $-.28$ for the electric utilities. Neither of these coefficients is significantly different from zero and the larger one even has the wrong sign.

[39]The tests consisted of fitting to the data the equation (19) of footnote 27. As shown there, it follows from the U-shaped hypothesis that the coefficient α of the variable $(D/V)^2/(1 - D/V)$, denoted hereafter by d^*, should be significant and positive. The following regression equations and partials were obtained:

Electric Utilities $\quad x = 5.0 + .017d - .003d^*; \ r_{xd^*.d} = -.15$

Oil Companies $\quad\quad x = 8.0 + .05d - .03d^*; \ r_{xd^*.d} = -.14.$

stock, $\bar{\pi}^{\tau}/S$, in any given class, should tend to increase with leverage as measured by the ratio D/S. The relation should tend to be linear and with positive slope through most of the relevant range (as in the curve MM' of Figure 2), though it might tend to flatten out if we move far enough to the right (as in the curve MD'), to the extent that high leverage tends to drive up the cost of senior capital. According to the conventional view, the yield curve as a function of leverage should be a horizontal straight line (like ML') through most of the relevant range; far enough to the right, the yield may tend to rise at an increasing rate. Here again, a straight-forward correlation—in this case between $\bar{\pi}^{\tau}/S$ and D/S—can provide a test of the two positions. If our view is correct, the correlation should be significantly positive; if the traditional view is correct, the correlation should be negligible.

Subject to the same qualifications noted above in connection with $\bar{X}^{\tau}$, we can approximate $\bar{\pi}^{\tau}$ by actual stockholder net income. [40] Letting z denote in each case the approximation to $\bar{\pi}^{\tau}/S$ (expressed as a percentage) and letting h denote the ratio D/S (also in percentage terms) the following results are obtained:

Electric Utilities $z = 6.6 + .017h \quad r = .53$
$\quad\quad\quad\quad\quad\quad\quad (+ .004)$

Oil Companies $z = 8.9 + .051h \quad r = .53.$
$\quad\quad\quad\quad\quad\quad\quad (\pm .012)$

These results are shown in scatter diagram form in Figures 5 and 6.

Here again the implications of our analysis seem to be borne out by the data. Both correlation coefficients are positive and highly significant when account is taken of the substantial sample size. Furthermore, the estimates of the coefficients of the equations seem to accord reasonably well with our

---

[40] As indicated earlier, Smith's data were for the single year 1953. Since the use of a single year's profits as a measure of expected profits might be open to objection we collected profit data for 1952 for the same companies and based the computation of $\bar{\pi}^{\tau}/S$ on the average of the two years. The value of $\bar{\pi}^{\tau}/S$ was obtained from the formula:

$$\left(\text{net earnings in 1952} \cdot \frac{\text{assets in '53}}{\text{assets in '52}} + \text{net earnings in '1953} \right)\frac{1}{2}$$

$$\div \text{ (average market value of common stock in '53).}$$

The asset adjustment was introduced as rough allowance for the effects of possible growth in the size of the firm. It might be added that the correlation computed with $\bar{\pi}^{\tau}/S$ based on net profits in 1953 alone was found to be only slightly smaller, namely .50.

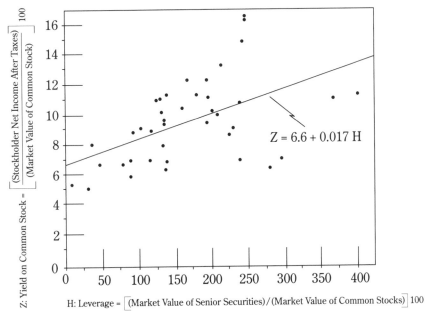

Figure 5   Yield on Common Stock in Relation to Leverage for 43 Electric Utilities, 1947–48

hypothesis. According to equation (12) the constant term should be the value of ρ_k^τ for the given class while the slope should be $(\rho_k^\tau - r)$. From the test of Proposition I we have seen that for the oil companies the mean value of ρ_k^τ could be estimated at around 8.7. Since the average yield of senior capital during the period covered was in the order of 3½ per cent, we should expect a constant term of about 8.7 per cent and a slope of just over 5 per cent. These values closely approximate the regression estimates of 8.9 per cent and 5.1 per cent respectively. For the electric utilities, the yield of senior capital was also on the order of 3½ per cent during the test years, but since the estimate of the mean value of ρ_k^τ from the test of Proposition I was 5.6 per cent, the slope should be just above 2 per cent. The actual regression estimate for the slope of 1.7 per cent is thus somewhat low, but still within one standard error of its theoretical value. Because of this underestimate of the slope and because of the large mean value of leverage ($\bar{h} = 160$ per cent) the regression estimate of the constant term, 6.6 per cent, is somewhat high, although not significantly different from the value of 5.6 per cent obtained in the test of Proposition I.

When we add a square term to the above equations to test for the presence and direction of curvature we obtain the following estimates:

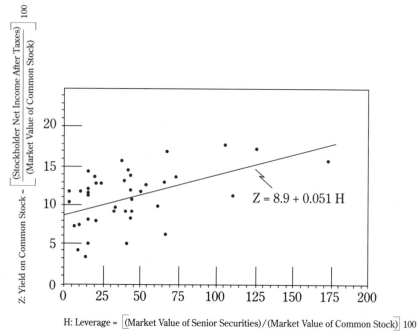

$$Z = 8.9 + 0.051\ H$$

H: Leverage = $\left[(\text{Market Value of Senior Securities}) / (\text{Market Value of Common Stock})\right] 100$

Figure 6   Yield on Common Stock in Relation to Leverage for 42 Oil Companies, 1952–53

Electric Utilities $z = 4.6 + .004h - .007h^2$

Oil Companies $z = 8.5 + .072h - .016h^2$.

For both cases the curvature is negative. In fact, for the electric utilities, where the observations cover a wider range of leverage ratios, the negative coefficient of the square term is actually significant at the 5 per cent level. Negative curvature, as we have seen, runs directly counter to the traditional hypothesis, whereas it can be readily accounted for by our model in terms of rising cost of borrowed funds. [41]

In summary, the empirical evidence we have reviewed seems to be broadly consistent with our model and largely inconsistent with traditional views. Needless to say much more extensive testing will be required before we

---

[41] That the yield of senior capital tended to rise for utilities as leverage increased is clearly shown in several of the scatter diagrams presented in the published version of Allen's study. This significant negative curvature between stock yields and leverage for utilities may be partly responsible for the fact, previously noted, that the constant in the linear regression is somewhat higher and the slope somewhat lower than implied by equation (12). Note also in connection with the estimate of ρ_k^{τ} that the introduction of the quadratic term reduces the constant considerably, pushing it in fact below the a priori expectation of 5.6, though the difference is again not statistically significant.

can firmly conclude that our theory describes market behavior. Caution is indicated especially with regard to our test of Proposition II, partly because of possible statistical pitfalls[42] and partly because not all the factors that might have a systematic effect on stock yields have been considered. In particular, no attempt was made to test the possible influence of the dividend pay-out ratio whose role has tended to receive a great deal of attention in current research and thinking. There are two reasons for this omission. First, our main objective has been to assess the prima facie tenability of *our* model, and in this model, based as it is on rational behavior by investors, dividends per se play no role. Second, in a world in which the policy of dividend stabilization is widespread, there is no simple way of disentangling the true effect of dividend payments on stock prices from their apparent effect, the latter reflecting only the role of dividends as a proxy measure of long-term earning anticipations.[43] The difficulties just mentioned are further compounded by possible interrelations between dividend policy and leverage.[44]

II.   Implications of the Analysis for the Theory of Investment

A.   *Capital Structure and Investment Policy*

On the basis of our propositions with respect to cost of capital and financial structure (and for the moment neglecting taxes), we can derive the following simple rule for optimal investment policy by the firm:

Proposition III. If a firm in class k is acting in the best interest of the stockholders at the time of the decision, it will exploit an investment opportunity if and only if the rate of return on the investment, say ρ^*, is as large as or larger

---

[42]In our test, *e.g.*, the two variables z and h are both ratios with S appearing in the denominator, which may tend to impart a positive bias to the correlation (*cf.* note 38). Attempts were made to develop alternative tests, but although various possibilities were explored, we have so far been unable to find satisfactory alternatives.

[43]We suggest that failure to appreciate this difficulty is responsible for many fallacious, or at least unwarranted, conclusions about the role of dividends.

[44]In the sample of electric utilities, there is a substantial negative correlation between yields and pay-out ratios, but also between pay-out ratios and leverage, suggesting that either the association of yields and leverage or of yields and pay-out ratios may be (at least partly) spurious. These difficulties however do not arise in the case of the oil industry sample. A preliminary analysis indicates that there is here no significant relation between leverage and pay-out ratios and also no significant correlation (either gross or partial) between yields and pay-out ratios.

than ρ_k. That is, *the cut-off point for investment in the firm will in all cases be ρ_k and will be completely unaffected by the type of security used to finance the investment.* Equivalently, we may say that regardless of the financing used, the marginal cost of capital to a firm is equal to the average cost of capital, which is in turn equal to the capitalization rate for an unlevered stream in the class to which the firm belongs. [45]

To establish this result we will consider the three major financing alternatives open to the firm—bonds, retained earnings, and common stock issues—and show that in each case an investment is worth undertaking if, and only if, $\rho^* \geq \rho_k$. [46]

Consider first the case of an investment financed by the sale of bonds. We know from Proposition I that the market value of the firm before the investment was undertaken was: [47]

$$V_0 = \overline{X}_0/\rho_k \tag{20}$$

and that the value of the common stock was:

$$S_0 = V_0 - D_0. \tag{21}$$

If now the firm borrows I dollars to finance an investment yielding ρ^* its market value will become:

$$V_1 = \frac{\overline{X}_0 + \rho^* I}{\rho_k} = V_0 + \frac{\rho^* I}{\rho_k} \tag{22}$$

and the value of its common stock will be:

$$S_1 = V_1 - (D_0 + I) = V_0 + \frac{\rho^* I}{\rho_k} - D_0 - I \tag{23}$$

or using equation 21,

---

[45] The analysis developed in this paper is essentially a comparative-statics, not a dynamic analysis. This note of caution applies with special force to Proposition III. Such problems as those posed by expected changes in r and in ρ_k over time will not be treated here. Although they are in principle amenable to analysis within the general framework we have laid out, such an undertaking is sufficiently complex to deserve separate treatment. *Cf.* note 17.

[46] The extension of the proof to other types of financing, such as the sale of preferred stock or the issuance of stock rights is straightforward.

[47] Since no confusion is likely to arise, we have again, for simplicity, eliminated the subscripts identifying the firm in the equations to follow. Except for ρ_k, the subscripts now refer to time periods.

$$S_1 = S_0 + \frac{\rho^* I}{\rho_k} - I. \tag{24}$$

Hence $S_1 \gtreqless S_0$ as $\rho^* \gtreqless \rho_k$.[48]

To illustrate, suppose the capitalization rate for uncertain streams in the kth class is 10 per cent and the rate of interest is 4 per cent. Then if a given company had an expected income of 1,000 and if it were financed entirely by common stock we know from Proposition I that the market value of its stock would be 10,000. Assume now that the managers of the firm discover an investment opportunity which will require an outlay of 100 and which is expected to yield 8 per cent. At first sight this might appear to be a profitable opportunity since the expected return is double the interest cost. If, however, the management borrows the necessary 100 at 4 per cent, the total expected income of the company rises to 1,008 and the market value of the firm to 10,080. But the firm now will have 100 of bonds in its capital structure so that, paradoxically, the market value of the stock must actually be reduced from 10,000 to 9,980 as a consequence of this apparently profitable investment. Or, to put it another way, the gains from being able to tap cheap, borrowed funds are more than offset for the stockholders by the market's discounting of the stock for the added leverage assumed.

Consider next the case of retained earnings. Suppose that in the course of its operations the firm acquired I dollars of cash (without impairing the earning power of its assets). If the cash is distributed as a dividend to the stockholders their wealth W_0, after the distribution will be:

$$W_0 = S_0 + I = \frac{\overline{X}_0}{\rho_k} - D_0 + I \tag{25}$$

where $\overline{X}_0$ represents the expected return from the assets exclusive of the amount I in question. If however the funds are retained by the company and

---

[48] In the case of bond-financing the rate of interest on bonds does not enter explicitly into the decision (assuming the firm borrows at the market rate of interest). This is true, moreover, given the conditions outlined in Section I.C, even though interest rates may be an increasing function of debt outstanding. To the extent that the firm borrowed at a rate other than the market rate the two I's in equation (24) would no longer be identical and an additional gain or loss, as the case might be, would accrue to the shareholders. It might also be noted in passing that permitting the two I's in (24) to take on different values provides a simple method for introducing underwriting expenses into the analysis.

used to finance new assets whose expected rate of return is ρ^*, then the stockholders' wealth would become:

$$W_1 = S_1 = \frac{\overline{X}_0 + \rho^*I}{\rho_k} - D_0 = S_0 + \frac{\rho^*I}{\rho_k}. \tag{26}$$

Clearly $W_1 \gtreqless W_0$ as $\rho^* \gtreqless \rho_k$ so that an investment financed by retained earnings raises the net worth of the owners if and only if $\rho^* > \rho_k$.[49]

Consider finally, the case of common-stock financing. Let P_0 denote the current market price per share of stock and assume, for simplicity, that this price reflects currently expected earnings only, that is, it does not reflect any future increase in earnings as a result of the investment under consideration.[50] Then if N is the original number of shares, the price per share is:

$$P_0 = S_0/N \tag{27}$$

and the number of new shares, M, needed to finance an investment of I dollars is given by:

$$M = \frac{I}{P_0}. \tag{28}$$

As a result of the investment the market value of the stock becomes:

$$S_1 = \frac{\overline{X}_0 + \rho^*I}{\rho_k} - D_0 = S_0 + \frac{\rho^*I}{\rho_k} = NP_0 + \frac{\rho^*I}{\rho_k}$$

and the price per share:

$$P_1 = \frac{S_1}{N + M} = \frac{1}{N + M}\left[NP_0 + \frac{\rho^*I}{\rho_k}\right]. \tag{29}$$

---

[49]The conclusion that ρ_k is the cut-off point for investments financed from internal funds applies not only to undistributed net profits, but to depreciation allowances (and even to the funds represented by the current sale value of any asset or collection of assets). Since the owners can earn ρ_k by investing funds elsewhere in the class, partial or total liquidating distributions should be made whenever the firm cannot achieve a marginal internal rate of return equal to ρ_k.

[50]If we assumed that the market price of the stock did reflect the expected higher future earnings (as would be the case if our original set of assumptions above were strictly followed) the analysis would differ slightly in detail, but not in essentials. The cut-off point for new investment would still be ρ_k, but where $\rho^* > \rho_k$ the gain to the original owners would be larger than if the stock price were based on the pre-investment expectations only.

Since by equation (28), $I = MP_0$, we can add MP_0 and subtract I from the quantity in bracket, obtaining:

$$P_1 = \frac{1}{N+M}\left[(N+M)P_0 + \frac{\rho^* - \rho_k}{\rho_k}I\right] \qquad (30)$$

$$= P_0 + \frac{1}{N+M}\frac{\rho^* - \rho_k}{\rho_k}I > P_0 \quad \text{if, and only if, } \rho^* > \rho_k.$$

Thus an investment financed by common stock is advantageous to the current stockholders if and only if its yield exceeds the capitalization rate ρ_k.

Once again a numerical example may help to illustrate the result and make it clear why the relevant cut-off rate is ρ_k and not the current yield on common stock, i. Suppose that ρ_k is 10 per cent, r is 4 per cent, that the original expected income of our company is 1,000 and that management has the opportunity of investing 100 having an expected yield of 12 per cent. If the original capital structure is 50 per cent debt and 50 per cent equity, and 1,000 shares of stock are initially outstanding, then, by Proposition I, the market value of the common stock must be 5,000 or 5 per share. Furthermore, since the interest bill is .04 × 5,000 = 200, the yield on common stock is 800/5,000 = 16 per cent. It may then appear that financing the additional investment of 100 by issuing 20 shares to outsiders at 5 per share would dilute the equity of the original owners since the 100 promises to yield 12 per cent whereas the common stock is currently yielding 16 per cent. Actually, however, the income of the company would rise to 1,012; the value of the firm to 10,120; and the value of the common stock to 5,120. Since there are now 1,020 shares, each would be worth 5.02 and the wealth of the original stockholders would thus have been increased. What has happened is that the dilution in expected earnings per share (from .80 to .796) has been more than offset, in its effect upon the market price of the shares, by the decrease in leverage.

Our conclusion is, once again, at variance with conventional views,[51] so much so as to be easily misinterpreted. Read hastily, Proposition III seems to imply that the capital structure of a firm is a matter of indifference; and that,

---

[51]In the matter of investment policy under uncertainty there is no single position which represents "accepted" doctrine. For a sample of current formulations, all very different from ours, see Joel Dean [2, esp. Ch. 3], M. Gordon and E. Shapiro [5], and Harry Roberts [17].

consequently, one of the core problems of corporate finance—the problem of the optimal capital structure for a firm—is no problem at all. It may be helpful, therefore, to clear up such possible misunderstandings.

B. *Proposition III and Financial Planning by Firms*

Misinterpretation of the scope of Proposition III can be avoided by remembering that this Proposition tells us only that the type of instrument used to finance an investment is irrelevant to the question of whether or not the investment is worth while. This does not mean that the owners (or the managers) have no grounds whatever for preferring one financing plan to another; or that there are no other policy or technical issues in finance at the level of the firm.

That grounds for preferring one type of financial structure to another will still exist within the framework of our model can readily be seen for the case of common-stock financing. In general, except for something like a widely publicized oil-strike, we would expect the market to place very heavy weight on current and recent past earnings in forming expectations as to future returns. Hence, if the owners of a firm discovered a major investment opportunity which they felt would yield much more than ρ_k, they might well prefer not to finance it via common stock at the then ruling price, because this price may fail to capitalize the new venture. A better course would be a pre-emptive issue of stock (and in this connection it should be remembered that stockholders are free to borrow and buy). Another possibility would be to finance the project initially with debt. Once the project had reflected itself in increased actual earnings, the debt could be retired either with an equity issue at much better prices or through retained earnings. Still another possibility along the same lines might be to combine the two steps by means of a convertible debenture or preferred stock, perhaps with a progressively declining conversion rate. Even such a double-stage financing plan may possibly be regarded as yielding too large a share to outsiders since the new stockholders are, in effect, being given an interest in any similar opportunities the firm may discover in the future. If there is a reasonable prospect that even larger opportunities may arise in the near future and if there is some danger that borrowing now would preclude more borrowing later, the owners might find their interests best protected by splitting off the current opportunity into a separate subsidiary with independent financing. Clearly the problems involved in making the crucial estimates and in planning the optimal financial strategy are by no means trivial, even though they should have no bearing on the basic decision to invest (as long as $\rho^* \geqq \rho_k$).[52]

Another reason why the alternatives in financial plans may not be a matter of indifference arises from the fact that managers are concerned with more than simply furthering the interest of the owners. Such other objectives of the management—which need not be necessarily in conflict with those of the owners—are much more likely to be served by some types of financing arrangements than others. In many forms of borrowing agreements, for example, creditors are able to stipulate terms which the current management may regard as infringing on its prerogatives or restricting its freedom to maneuver. The creditors might even be able to insist on having a direct voice in the formation of policy.[53] To the extent, therefore, that financial policies have these implications for the management of the firm, something like the utility approach described in the introductory section becomes relevant to financial (as opposed to investment) decision-making. It is, however, the utility functions of the managers per se and not of the owners that are now involved.[54]

In summary, many of the specific considerations which bulk so large in traditional discussions of corporate finance can readily be superimposed on our sample framework without forcing any drastic (and certainly no systematic) alteration of the conclusion which is our principal concern, namely that for investment decisions, the marginal cost of capital is ρ_k.

---

[52]Nor can we rule out the possibility that the existing owners, if unable to use a financing plan which protects their interest, may actually prefer to pass up an otherwise profitable venture rather than give outsiders an "excessive" share of the business. It is presumably in situations of this kind that we could justifiably speak of a shortage of "equity capital," though this kind of market imperfection is likely to be of significance only for small or new firms.

[53]Similar considerations are involved in the matter of dividend policy. Even though the stockholders may be indifferent as to payout policy as long as investment policy is optimal, the management need not be so. Retained earnings involve far fewer threats to control than any of the alternative sources of funds and, of course, involve no underwriting expense or risk. But against these advantages management must balance the fact that sharp changes in dividend rates, which heavy reliance on retained earnings might imply, may give the impression that a firm's finances are being poorly managed, with consequent threats to the control and professional standing of the management.

[54]In principle, at least, this introduction of management's risk preferences with respect to financing methods would do much to reconcile the apparent conflict between Proposition III and such empirical findings as those of Modigliani and Zeman [14] on the close relation between interest rates and the ratio of new debt to new equity issues; or of John Lintner [12] on the considerable stability in target and actual dividend-payout ratios.

C.   *The Effect of the Corporate Income Tax on Investment Decisions*

In Section I it was shown that when an unintegrated corporate income tax is introduced, the original version of our Proposition I,

$$\overline{X}/V = \rho_k = \text{ a constant}$$

must be rewritten as:

$$\frac{(\overline{X} - rD)(1 - \tau) + rD}{V} \equiv \frac{\overline{X}^\tau}{V} = \rho_k^\tau = \text{ a constant.} \tag{11}$$

Throughout Section I we found it convenient to refer to $\overline{X}^\tau/V$ as the cost of capital. The appropriate measure of the cost of capital relevant to investment decisions, however, is the ratio of the expected return *before* taxes to the market value, *i.e.*, $\overline{X}/V$. From (11) above we find:

$$\frac{\overline{X}}{V} = \frac{\rho_k^\tau - \tau_r(D/V)}{1 - \tau} = \frac{\rho_k^\tau}{1 - \tau}\left[1 - \frac{\tau r D}{\rho_k^\tau V}\right], \tag{31}$$

which shows that the cost of capital now depends on the debt ratio, decreasing, as D/V rises, at the constant rate $\tau r/(1 - \tau)$. [55] Thus, with a corporate income tax under which interest is a deductible expense, gains can accrue to stockholders from having debt in the capital structure, even when capital markets are perfect. The gains however are small, as can be seen from (31), and as will be shown more explicitly below.

From (31) we can develop the tax-adjusted counterpart of Proposition III by interpreting the term D/V in that equation as the proportion of debt used in any additional financing of V dollars. For example, in the case where the

---

[55] Equation (31) is amenable, in principle, to statistical tests similar to those described in Section I.E. However, we have not made any systematic attempt to carry out such tests so far, because neither the Allen nor the Smith study provides the required information. Actually, Smith's data included a very crude estimate of tax liability, and, using this estimate, we did in fact obtain a negative relation between $\overline{X}/V$ and D/V. However, the correlation $(-.28)$ turned out to be significant only at about the 10 per cent level. While this result is not conclusive, it should be remembered that, according to our theory, the slope of the regression equation should be in any event quite small. In fact, with a value of τ in the order of .5, and values of ρ_k^τ and r in the order of 8.5 and 3.5 per cent respectively (*cf.* Section I.E) an increase in D/V from 0 to 60 per cent (which is, approximately, the range of variation of this variable in the sample) should tend to reduce the average cost of capital only from about 17 to about 15 per cent.

financing is entirely by new common stock, $D = 0$ and the required rate of return ρ_k^S on a venture so financed becomes:

$$\rho_k^S = \frac{\rho_k^\tau}{1 - \tau}. \tag{32}$$

For the other extreme of pure debt financing $D = V$ and the required rate of return, ρ_k^D, becomes:

$$\rho_k^D = \frac{\rho_k^\tau}{1 - \tau}\left[1 - \tau \frac{r}{\rho_k^\tau}\right] = \rho_k^S\left[1 - \tau \frac{r}{\rho_k^\tau}\right] = \rho_k^S - \frac{\tau}{1 - \tau}r. \; ^{56} \tag{33}$$

For investments financed out of retained earnings, the problem of defining the required rate of return is more difficult since it involves a comparison of the tax consequences to the individual stockholder of receiving a dividend versus having a capital gain. Depending on the time of realization, a capital gain produced by retained earnings may be taxed either at ordinary income tax rates, 50 per cent of these rates, 25 per cent, or zero, if held till death. The rate on any dividends received in the event of a distribution will also be a variable depending on the amount of other income received by the stockholder, and with the added complications introduced by the current dividend-credit provisions. If we assume that the managers proceed on the basis of reasonable estimates as to the average values of the relevant tax rates for the owners, then the required return for retained earnings ρ_k^R can be shown to be:

$$\rho_k^R = \rho_k^\tau \frac{1}{1 - \tau}\frac{1 - \tau_d}{1 - \tau_g} = \frac{1 - \tau_d}{1 - \tau_g}\rho_k^S \tag{34}$$

where τ_d is the assumed rate of personal income tax on dividends and τ_g is the assumed rate of tax on capital gains.

A numerical illustration may perhaps be helpful in clarifying the relationship between these required rates of return. If we take the following round numbers as representative order-of-magnitude values under present conditions: an after-tax capitalization rate ρ_k^τ of 10 per cent, a rate of interest on

---

[56]This conclusion does not extend to preferred stocks even though they have been classed with debt issues previously. Since preferred dividends except for a portion of those of public utilities are not in general deductible from the corporate tax, the cut-off point for new financing via preferred stock is exactly the same as that for common stock.

bonds of 4 per cent, a corporate tax rate of 50 per cent, a marginal personal income tax rate on dividends of 40 per cent (corresponding to an income of about $25,000 on a joint return), and a capital gains rate of 20 per cent (one-half the marginal rate on dividends), then the required rates of return would be: (1) 20 per cent for investments financed entirely by issuance of new common shares; (2) 16 per cent for investments financed entirely by new debt; and (3) 15 per cent for investments financed wholly from internal funds.

These results would seem to have considerable significance for current discussions of the effect of the corporate income tax on financial policy and on investment. Although we cannot explore the implications of the results in any detail here, we should at least like to call attention to the remarkably small difference between the "cost" of equity funds and debt funds. With the numerical values assumed, equity money turned out to be only 25 per cent more expensive than debt money, rather than something on the order of 5 times as expensive as is commonly supposed to be the case. [57] The reason for the wide difference is that the traditional view starts from the position that debt funds are several times cheaper than equity funds even in the absence of taxes, with taxes serving simply to magnify the cost ratio in proportion to the corporate rate. By contrast, in our model in which the repercussions of debt financing on the value of shares are taken into account, the *only* difference in cost is that due to the tax effect, and its magnitude is simply the tax on the "grossed up" interest payment. Not only is this magnitude likely to be small but our analysis yields the further paradoxical implication that the stockholders' gain from, and hence incentive to use, debt financing is actually smaller the lower the rate of interest. In the extreme case where the firm could borrow for practically nothing, the advantage of debt financing would also be practically nothing.

---

[57] See *e.g.*, D. T. Smith [18]. It should also be pointed out that our tax system acts in other ways to reduce the gains from debt financing. Heavy reliance on debt in the capital structure, for example, commits a company to paying out a substantial proportion of its income in the form of interest payments taxable to the owners under the personal income tax. A debt-free company, by contrast, can reinvest in the business all of its (smaller) net income and to this extent subject the owners only to the low capital gains rate (or possibly no tax at all by virtue of the loophole at death). Thus, we should expect a high degree of leverage to be of value to the owners, even in the case of closely held corporations, primarily in cases where their firm was not expected to have much need for additional funds to expand assets and earnings in the future. To the extent that opportunities for growth were available, as they presumably would be for most successful corporations, the interest of the stockholders would tend to be better served by a structure which permitted maximum use of retained earnings.

III.   Conclusion

With the development of Proposition III the main objectives we outlined in our introductory discussion have been reached. We have in our Propositions I and II at least the foundations of a theory of the valuation of firms and shares in a world of uncertainty. We have shown, moreover, how this theory can lead to an operational definition of the cost of capital and how that concept can be used in turn as a basis for rational investment decision-making within the firm. Needless to say, however, much remains to be done before the cost of capital can be put away on the shelf among the solved problems. Our approach has been that of static, partial equilibrium analysis. It has assumed among other things a state of atomistic competition in the capital markets and an ease of access to those markets which only a relatively small (though important) group of firms even come close to possessing. These and other drastic simplifications have been necessary in order to come to grips with the problem at all. Having served their purpose they can now be relaxed in the direction of greater realism and relevance, a task in which we hope others interested in this area wish to share.

References

1. F. B. Allen, "Does Going into Debt Lower the 'Cost of Capital'?," *Analysts Jour.*, Aug. 1954, 10, 57–61.

2. J. Dean, *Capital Budgeting*. New York 1951.

3. D. Durand, "Costs of Debt and Equity Funds for Business: Trends and Problems of Measurement" in Nat. Bur. Econ. Research, *Conference on Research in Business Finance*. New York 1952, pp. 215–47.

4. W. J. Eiteman, "Financial Aspects of Promotion," in *Essays on Business Finance* by M. W. Waterford and W. J. Eiteman. Ann Arbor, Mich. 1952, pp. 1–17.

5. M. J. Gordon and E. Shapiro, "Capital Equipment Analysis: The Required Rate of Profit," *Manag. Sci.*, Oct. 1956, 3, 102–10.

6. B. Graham and L. Dodd, *Security Analysis*, 3rd ed. New York 1951.

7. G. Guthmann and H. E. Dougall, *Corporate Financial Policy*, 3rd ed. New York 1955.

8. J. R. Hicks, *Value and Capital*, 2nd ed. Oxford 1946.

9. P. Hunt and M. Williams, *Case Problems in Finance*, rev. ed. Homewood, Ill. 1954.

10. J. M. Keynes, *The General Theory of Employment, Interest and Money*. New York 1936.

11. O. Lange, *Price Flexibility and Employment*. Bloomington, Ind. 1944.

12. J. Lintner, "Distribution of Incomes of Corporations among Dividends, Retained Earnings and Taxes," *Am. Econ. Rev.*, May 1956, 46, 97–113.

13. F. Lutz and V. Lutz, *The Theory of Investment of the Firm*. Princeton 1951.

14. F. Modigliani and M. Zeman, "The Effect of the Availability of Funds, and the Terms Thereof, on Business Investment" in Nat. Bur. Econ. Research, *Conference on Research in Business Finance*. New York 1952, pp. 263–309.

15. W. A. Morton, "The Structure of the Capital Market and the Price of Money," *Am. Econ. Rev.*, May 1954, 44, 440–54.

16. S. M. Robbins, *Managing Securities*. Boston 1954.

17. H. V. Roberts, "Current Problems in the Economics of Capital Budgeting," *Jour. Bus.*, 1957, 30 (1), 12–16.

18. D. T. Smith, *Effects of Taxation on Corporate Financial Policy*. Boston 1952.

19. R. Smith, "Cost of Capital in the Oil Industry," (hectograph). Pittsburgh: Carnegie Inst. Tech. 1955.

20. H. M. Somers, " 'Cost of Money' as the Determinant of Public Utility Rates," *Buffalo Law Rev.*, Spring 1955, 4, 1–28.

21. J. B. Williams, *The Theory of Investment Value*. Cambridge, Mass. 1938.

22. U. S. Federal Communications Commission, *The Problem of the "Rate of Return" in Public Utility Regulation*. Washington 1938.

Dividend Policy, Growth, and the Valuation of Shares*

Merton H. Miller† and Franco Modigliani‡

The effect of a firm's dividend policy on the current price of its shares is a matter of considerable importance, not only to the corporate officials who must set the policy, but to investors planning portfolios and to economists seeking to understand and appraise the functioning of the capital markets. Do companies with generous distribution policies consistently sell at a premium over those with niggardly payouts? Is the reverse ever true? If so, under what conditions? Is there an optimum payout ratio or range of ratios that maximizes the current worth of the shares?

Although these questions of fact have been the subject of many empirical studies in recent years no consensus has yet been achieved. One reason appears to be the absence in the literature of a complete and reasonably rigorous statement of those parts of the economic theory of valuation bearing directly on the matter of dividend policy. Lacking such a statement, investigators have not yet been able to frame their test with sufficient precision to

*The authors wish to express their thanks to all who read and commented on earlier versions of this paper and especially to Charles C. Holt, now of the University of Wisconsin, whose suggestions led to considerable simplification of a number of the proofs.

†Professor of finance and economics, University of Chicago.

‡Professor of economics, Northwestern University.

distinguish adequately between the various contending hypotheses. Nor have they been able to give a convincing explanation of what their test results do imply about the underlying process of valuation.

In the hope that it may help to overcome these obstacles to effective empirical testing, this paper will attempt to fill the existing gap in the theoretical literature on valuation. We shall begin, in Section I, by examining the effects of differences in dividend policy on the current price of shares in an ideal economy characterized by perfect capital markets, rational behavior, and perfect certainty. Still within this convenient analytical framework we shall go on in Sections II and III to consider certain closely related issues that appear to have been responsible for considerable misunderstanding of the role of dividend policy. In particular, Section II will focus on the long-standing debate about what investors "really" capitalize when they buy shares; and Section III on the much mooted relations between price, the rate of growth of profits, and the rate of growth of dividends per share. Once these fundamentals have been established, we shall proceed in Section IV to drop the assumption of certainty and to see the extent to which the earlier conclusions about dividend policy must be modified. Finally, in Section V, we shall briefly examine the implications for the dividend policy problem of certain kinds of market imperfections.

I. Effect of Dividend Policy with Perfect Markets, Rational Behavior, and Perfect Certainty

The meaning of the basic assumptions.—Although the terms "perfect markets," "rational behavior," and "perfect certainty" are widely used throughout economic theory, it may be helpful to start by spelling out the precise meaning of these assumptions in the present context.

1. In "perfect capital markets," no buyer or seller (or issuer) of securities is large enough for his transactions to have an appreciable impact on the then ruling price. All traders have equal and costless access to information about the ruling price and about all other relevant characteristics of shares (to be detailed specifically later). No brokerage fees, transfer taxes, or other transaction costs are incurred when securities are bought, sold, or issued, and there are no tax differentials either between distributed and undistributed profits or between dividends and capital gains.

2. "Rational behavior" means that investors always prefer more wealth to less and are indifferent as to whether a given increment to their wealth takes

the form of cash payments or an increase in the market value of their holdings of shares.

3. "Perfect certainty" implies complete assurance on the part of every investor as to the future investment program and the future profits of every corporation. Because of this assurance, there is, among other things, no need to distinguish between stocks and bonds as sources of funds at this stage of the analysis. We can, therefore, proceed as if there were only a single type of financial instrument which, for convenience, we shall refer to as shares of stock.

The fundamental principle of valuation.—Under these assumptions the valuation of all shares would be governed by the following fundamental principle: the price of each share must be such that the rate of return (dividends plus capital gains per dollar invested) on every share will be the same throughout the market over any given interval of time. That is, if we let

$d_j(t)$ = dividends per share paid by firm j during period t

$p_j(t)$ = the price (ex any dividend in $t - 1$) of a share in firm j at the start of period t,

we must have

$$\frac{d_j(t) + p_j(t + 1) - p_j(t)}{p_j(t)} = \rho(t) \quad \text{independent of } j; \tag{1}$$

or, equivalently,

$$p_j(t) = \frac{1}{1 + \rho(t)} [d_j(t) + p_j(t + 1)] \tag{2}$$

for each j and for all t. Otherwise, holders of low-return (high-priced) shares could increase their terminal wealth by selling these shares and investing the proceeds in shares offering a higher rate of return. This process would tend to drive down the prices of the low-return shares and drive up the prices of high-return shares until the differential in rates of return had been eliminated.

The effect of dividend policy.—The implications of this principle for our problem of dividend policy can be seen somewhat more easily if equation (2) is restated in terms of the value of the enterprise as a whole rather than in terms of the value of an individual share. Dropping the firm subscript j since this will lead to no ambiguity in the present context and letting

151

$n(t)$ = the number of shares of record at the start of t

$m(t + 1)$ = the number of new shares (if any) sold during t at the ex dividend closing price $p(t + 1)$, so that

$n(t + 1) = n(t) + m(t + 1)$

$V(t) = n(t)p(t)$ = the total value of the enterprise and

$D(t) = n(t)d(t)$ = the total dividends paid during t to holders of record at the start of t,

we can rewrite (2)

$$V(t) = \frac{1}{1 + \rho(t)} [D(t) + n(t)p(t + 1)]$$

$$= \frac{1}{1 + \rho(t)} [D(t) + V(t + 1) - m(t + 1)p(t + 1)]. \tag{3}$$

The advantage of restating the fundamental rule in this form is that it brings into sharper focus the three possible routes by which current dividends might affect the current market value of the firm $V(t)$, or equivalently the price of its individual shares, $p(t)$. Current dividends will clearly affect $V(t)$ via the first term in the bracket, $D(t)$. In principle, current dividends might also affect $V(t)$ indirectly via the second term, $V(t + 1)$, the new ex dividend market value. Since $V(t + 1)$ must depend only on future and not on past events, such could be the case, however, only if both (a) $V(t + 1)$ were a function of future dividend policy and (b) the current distribution $D(t)$ served to convey some otherwise unavailable information as to what that future dividend policy would be. The first possibility being the relevant one from the standpoint of assessing the effects of dividend policy, it will clarify matters to assume, provisionally, that the future dividend policy of the firm is known and given for $t + 1$ and all subsequent periods and is independent of the actual dividend decision in t. Then $V(t + 1)$ will also be independent of the current dividend decision, though it may very well be affected by $D(t + 1)$ and all subsequent distributions. Finally, current dividends can influence $V(t)$ through the third term, $-m(t + 1)p(t + 1)$, the value of new shares sold to outsiders during the period. For the higher the dividend payout in any period the more the new capital that must be raised from external sources to maintain any desired level of investment.

The fact that the dividend decision effects [*sic*] price not in one but in these two conflicting ways—directly via $D(t)$ and inversely via $-m(t)p(t + 1)$—is, of course, precisely why one speaks of there being a dividend policy *problem.* If the firm raises its dividend in t, given its investment decision, will the increase in the cash payments to the current holders be more or less than enough to offset their lower share of the terminal value? Which is the better strategy for the firm in financing the investment: to reduce dividends and rely on retained earnings or to raise dividends but float more new shares?

In our ideal world at least these and related questions can be simply and immediately answered: the two dividend effects must always exactly cancel out so that the payout policy to be followed in t will have *no* effect on the price at t.

We need only express $m(t + 1) \cdot p(t + 1)$ in terms of $D(t)$ to show that such must indeed be the case. Specifically, if $I(t)$ is the given level of the firm's investment or increase in its holding of physical assets in t and if $X(t)$ is the firm's total net profit for the period, we know that the amount of outside capital required will be

$$m(t + 1)p(t + 1) = I(t) - [X(t) - D(t)]. \tag{4}$$

Substituting expression (4) into (3), the $D(t)$ cancel and we obtain for the value of the firm as of the start of t

$$V(t) \equiv n(t)p(t) = \frac{1}{1 + \rho(t)} [X(t) - I(t) + V(t + 1)]. \tag{5}$$

Since $D(t)$ does not appear directly among the arguments and since $X(t)$, $I(t)$, $V(t + 1)$ and $\rho(t)$ are all independent of $D(t)$ (either by their nature or by assumption) it follows that the current value of the firm must be independent of the current dividend decision.

Having established that $V(t)$ is unaffected by the current dividend decision it is easy to go on to show that $V(t)$ must also be unaffected by any future dividend decisions as well. Such future decisions can influence $V(t)$ only via their effect on $V(t + 1)$. But we can repeat the reasoning above and show that $V(t + 1)$—and hence $V(t)$—is unaffected by dividend policy in $t + 1$; that $V(t + 2)$—and hence $V(t + 1)$ and $V(t)$—is unaffected by dividend policy in $t + 2$; and so on for as far into the future as we care to look. Thus, we may conclude that given a firm's investment policy, the dividend payout policy it chooses to follow will affect neither the current price of its shares nor the total return to its shareholders.

Like many other propositions in economics, the irrelevance of dividend policy, given investment policy, is "obvious, once you think of it." It is, after all, merely one more instance of the general principle that there are no "financial illusions" in a rational and perfect economic environment. Values there are determined solely by "real" considerations—in this case the earning power of the firm's assets and its investment policy—and not by how the fruits of the earning power are "packaged" for distribution.

Obvious as the proposition may be, however, one finds few references to it in the extensive literature on the problem.[1] It is true that the literature abounds with statements that in some "theoretical" sense, dividend policy ought not to count; but either that sense is not clearly specified or, more frequently and especially among economists, it is (wrongly) identified with a situation in which the firm's internal rate of return is the same as the external or market rate of return.[2]

A major source of these and related misunderstandings of the role of the dividend policy has been the fruitless concern and controversy over what investors "really" capitalize when they buy shares. We say fruitless because as we shall now proceed to show, it is actually possible to derive from the basic principle of valuation (1) not merely one, but several valuation formulas each starting from one of the "classical" views of what is being capitalized by investors. Though differing somewhat in outward appearance, the various formulas can be shown to be equivalent in all essential respects including, of course, their implication that dividend policy is irrelevant. While the controversy [sic] itself thus turns out to be an empty one, the different expressions do have some intrinsic interest since, by highlighting different combinations of variables they provide additional insights into the process of valuation and they open alternative lines of attack on some of the problems of empirical testing.

II.   What Does the Market "Really" Capitalize?

In the literature on valuation one can find at least the following four more or less distinct approaches to the valuation of shares: (1) the discounted cash flow approach; (2) the current earnings plus future investment opportunities approach; (3) the stream of dividends approach; and (4) the stream of earnings approach. To demonstrate that these approaches are, in fact, equivalent it will

---

[1] Apart from the references to it in our earlier papers, especially [16], the closest approximation seems to be that in Bodenborn [sic] [1, p. 492], but even his treatment of the role of dividend policy is not completely explicit. (The numbers in brackets refer to references listed below, pp. 432–33.)

[2] See below p. 424.

be helpful to begin by first going back to equation (5) and developing from it a valuation formula to serve as a point of reference and comparison. Specifically, if we assume, for simplicity, that the market rate of yield $\rho(t) = \rho$ for all t,[3] then, setting $t = 0$, we can rewrite (5) as

$$V(0) = \frac{1}{1 + \rho} [X(0) - I(0)] + \frac{1}{1 + \rho} V(1). \tag{6}$$

Since (5) holds for all t, setting $t = 1$ permits us to express $V(1)$ in terms of $V(2)$ which in turn can be expressed in terms of $V(3)$ and so on up to any arbitrary terminal period T. Carrying out these substitutions, we obtain

$$V(0) = \sum_{t=0}^{T-1} \frac{1}{(1 + \rho)^{t+1}} [X(t) - I(t)] + \frac{1}{(1 + \rho)^T} V(T). \tag{7}$$

In general, the remainder term $(1 + \rho)^{-T} \cdot V(T)$ can be expected to approach zero as T approaches infinity[4] so that (7) can be expressed as

$$V(0) = \lim_{T \to \infty} \sum_{t=0}^{T-1} \frac{1}{(1 + \rho)^{t+1}} [X(t) - I(t)], \tag{8}$$

which we shall further abbreviate to

$$V(0) = \sum_{t=0}^{\infty} \frac{1}{(1 + \rho)^{t+1}} [X(t) - I(t)]. \tag{9}$$

The discounted cash flow approach.—Consider now the so-called discounted cash flow approach familiar in discussions of capital budgeting. There, in valuing any specific machine we discount at the market rate of interest the

---

[3]More general formulas in which $\rho(t)$ is allowed to vary with time can always be derived from those presented here merely by substituting the cumbersome product

$$\prod_{\tau=0}^{t} [1 + \rho(\tau)] \quad \text{for} \quad (1 + \rho)^{t+1}.$$

[4]The assumption that the remainder vanishes is introduced for the sake of simplicity of exposition only and is in no way essential to the argument. What is essential, of course, is that $V(0)$, i.e., the sum of the two terms in (7), be finite, but this can always be safely assumed in economic analysis. See below, n. 14.

stream of cash receipts generated by the machine; plus any scrap or terminal value of the machine; and minus the stream of cash outlays for direct labor, materials, repairs, and capital additions. The same approach, of course, can also be applied to the firm as a whole which may be thought of in this context as simply a large, composite machine.[5] This approach amounts to defining the value of the firm as

$$V(0) - \sum_{t=0}^{T-1} \frac{1}{(1+\rho)^{t+1}} [\mathcal{R}(t) - \mathcal{O}(t)] + \frac{1}{(1+\rho)^{T}} V(T), \tag{10}$$

where $\mathcal{R}(t)$ represents the stream of cash receipts and $\mathcal{O}(t)$ of cash outlays, or, abbreviating, as above, to

$$V(0) = \sum_{t=0}^{\infty} \frac{1}{(1+\rho)^{t+1}} [\mathcal{R}(t) - \mathcal{O}(t)]. \tag{11}$$

But we also know, by definition, that $[X(t) - I(t)] = [\mathcal{R}(t) - \mathcal{O}(t)]$ since, $X(t)$ differs from $\mathcal{R}(t)$ and $I(t)$ differs from $\mathcal{O}(t)$ merely by the "cost of goods sold" (and also by the depreciation expense if we wish to interpret $X(t)$ and $I(t)$ as net rather than gross profits and investment). Hence (11) is formally equivalent to (9), and the discounted cash flow approach is thus seen to be an implication of the valuation principle for perfect markets given by equation (1).

The investment opportunities approach.—Consider next the approach to valuation which would seem most natural from the standpoint of an investor proposing to buy out and operate some already-going concern. In estimating how much it would be worthwhile to pay for the privilege of operating the firm, the amount of dividends to be paid is clearly not relevant, since the new owner can, within wide limits, make the future dividend stream whatever he pleases. For him the worth of the enterprise, as such, will depend only on: (*a*) the "normal" rate of return he can earn by investing his capital in securities (i.e., the market rate of return); (*b*) the earning power of the physical assets currently held by the firm; and (*c*) the opportunities, if any, that the firm offers for making

---

[5]This is, in fact, the approach to valuation normally taken in economic theory when discussing the value of the *assets* of an enterprise, but much more rarely applied, unfortunately, to the value of the liability side. One of the few to apply the approach to the shares as well as the assets is Bodenhorn in [1], who uses it to derive a formula closely similar to (9) above.

additional investments in real assets that will yield more than the "normal" (market) rate of return. The latter opportunities, frequently termed the "good will" of the business, may arise, in practice, from any of a number of circumstances (ranging all the way from special locational advantages to patents or other monopolistic advantages).

To see how these opportunities affect the value of the business assume that in some future period t the firm invests $I(t)$ dollars. Suppose, further, for simplicity, that starting in the period immediately following the investment of the funds, the projects produce net profits at a constant rate of $\rho^*(t)$ per cent of $I(t)$ in each period thereafter.[6] Then the present worth as of t of the (perpetual) stream of profits generated will be $I(t)\rho^*(t)/\rho$, and the "good will" of the projects (i.e., the difference between worth and cost) will be

$$I(t)\frac{\rho^*(t)}{\rho} - I(t) = I(t)\left[\frac{\rho^*(t) - \rho}{\rho}\right].$$

The present worth as of now of this future "good will" is

$$I(t)\left[\frac{\rho^*(t) - \rho}{\rho}\right](1 + \rho)^{-(t+1)},$$

and the present value of all such future opportunities is simply the sum

$$\sum_{t=0}^{\infty} I(t)\frac{\rho^*(t) - \rho}{\rho}(1 + \rho)^{-(t+1)}.$$

Adding in the present value of the (uniform perpetual) earnings, $X(0)$, on the assets currently held, we get as an expression for the value of the firm

$$V(0) = \frac{X(0)}{\rho} + \sum_{t=0}^{\infty} I(t)\frac{\rho^*(t) - \rho}{\rho}(1 + \rho)^{-(t+1)}. \tag{12}$$

---

[6] The assumption that $I(t)$ yields a uniform perpetuity is not restrictive in the present certainty context since it is always possible by means of simple, present-value calculations to find an equivalent uniform perpetuity for any project, whatever the time shape of its actual returns. Note also that p*(t) is the *average* rate of return. If the managers of the firm are behaving rationally, they will, of course, use ρ as their cut-off criterion (cf. below p. 418). In this event we would have $\rho^*(t) \geq \rho$. The formulas remain valid, however, even where $\rho^*(t) < \rho$.

To show that the same formula can be derived from (9) note first that our definition of $\rho^*(t)$ implies the following relation between the $X(t)$:

$$X(1) = X(0) + \rho^*(0)I(0),$$

$$\cdots\cdots\cdots\cdots\cdots\cdots$$

$$X(t) = X(t-1) + \rho^*(t-1)I(t-1)$$

and by successive substitution

$$X(t) = X(0) + \sum_{\tau=0}^{t-1} \rho^*(\tau)I(\tau),$$

$$t = 1, 2, \ldots \infty.$$

Substituting the last expression for $X(t)$ in (9) yields

$$V(0) = [X(0) - I(0)](1+\rho)^{-1} + \sum_{t=1}^{\infty} \left[X(0) + \sum_{\tau=0}^{t-1} \rho^*(\tau)I(\tau) - I(t) \right]$$

$$\times (1+\rho)^{-(t+1)}$$

$$= X(0)\sum_{t=1}^{\infty}(1+\rho)^{-t} - I(0)(1+\rho)^{-1} + \sum_{t=1}^{\infty} \left[\sum_{\tau=0}^{t-1} \rho^*(\tau)I(\tau) - I(t) \right]$$

$$\times (1+\rho)^{-(t+1)}$$

$$= X(0)\sum_{t=1}^{\infty}(1+\rho)^{-t} + \sum_{t=1}^{\infty} \left[\sum_{\tau=0}^{t-1} \rho^*(\tau)I(\tau) - I(t-1) \times (1+\rho) \right]$$

$$\times (1+\rho)^{-(t+1)}.$$

The first expression is, of course, simply a geometric progression summing to $X(0)/\rho$, which is the first term of (12). To simplify the second expression note that it can be rewritten as

$$\sum_{t=0}^{\infty} I(t) \left[\rho^*(t) \sum_{\tau=t+2}^{\infty} (1+\rho)^{-\tau} - (1+\rho)^{-(t+1)} \right].$$

158

Evaluating the summation within the brackets gives

$$\sum_{t=0}^{\infty} I(t) \left[\rho^*(t) \frac{(1 + \rho)^{-(t+1)}}{\rho} - (1 + \rho)^{-(t+1)} \right]$$

$$= \sum_{t=0}^{\infty} I(t) \left[\frac{\rho^*(t) - \rho}{\rho} \right] (1 + \rho)^{-(t+1)},$$

which is precisely the second term of (12).

Formula (12) has a number of revealing features and deserves to be more widely used in discussions of valuation.[7] For one thing, it throws considerable light on the meaning of those much abused terms "growth" and "growth stocks." As can readily be seen from (12), a corporation does not become a "growth stock" with a high price–earnings ratio merely because its assets and earnings are growing over time. To enter the glamor category, it is also necessary that $\rho^*(t) > \rho$. For if $\rho^*(t) = \rho$, then however large the growth in assets may be, the second term in (12) will be zero and the firm's price–earnings ratio would not rise above a humdrum $1/\rho$. The essence of "growth," in short, is not expansion, but the existence of opportunities to invest significant quantities of funds at higher than "normal" rates of return.

Notice also that if $\rho^*(t) < \rho$, investment in real assets by the firm will actually reduce the current price of the shares. This should help to make clear among other things, why the "cost of capital" to the firm is the same regardless of how the investments are financed or how fast the firm is growing. The function of the cost of capital in capital budgeting is to provide the "cut-off rate" in the sense of the minimum yield that investment projects must promise to be worth undertaking from the point of view of the current owners. Clearly, no proposed project would be in the interest of the current owners if its yield were expected to be less than ρ since investing in such projects would reduce the value of their shares. In the other direction, every project yielding more than ρ is just as clearly worth undertaking since it will necessarily enhance the value of

---

[7] A valuation formula analogous to (12) though derived and interpreted in a slightly different way is found in Bodenhorn [1]. Variants of (12) for certain special cases are discussed in Walter [20].

the enterprise. Hence, the cost of capital or cut-off criterion for investment decisions is simply ρ. [8]

Finally, formula (12) serves to emphasize an important deficiency in many recent statistical studies of the effects of dividend policy (such as Walter [19] or Durand [4, 5]). These studies typically involve fitting regression equations in which price is expressed as some function of current earnings and dividends. A finding that the dividend coefficient is significant—as is usually the case—is then interpreted as a rejection of the hypothesis that dividend policy does not affect valuation.

Even without raising questions of bias in the coefficients, [9] it should be apparent that such a conclusion is unwarranted since formula (12) and the analysis underlying it imply only that dividends will not count given current earnings *and growth potential.* No general prediction is made (or can be made) by the theory about what will happen to the dividend coefficient if the crucial growth term is omitted. [10]

The stream of dividends approach.—From the earnings and earnings opportunities approach we turn next to the dividend approach, which has, for some reason, been by far the most popular one in the literature of valuation. This approach too, properly formulated, is an entirely valid one though, of course, not the only valid approach as its more enthusiastic proponents

---

[8] The same conclusion could also have been reached, of course, by "costing" each particular source of capital funds. That is, since ρ is the going market rate of return on equity any new shares floated to finance investment must be priced to yield ρ; and withholding funds from the stockholders to finance investment would deprive the holders of the chance to earn ρ on these funds by investing their dividends in other shares. The advantage of thinking in terms of the cost of capital as the cut-off criterion is that it minimizes the danger of confusing "costs" with mere "outlays."

[9] The serious bias problem in tests using current reported earnings as a measure of $X(0)$ was discussed briefly by us in [16].

[10] In suggesting that recent statistical studies have not controlled adequately for growth we do not mean to exempt Gordon in [8] or [9]. It is true that his tests contain an explicit "growth" variable, but it is essentially nothing more than the ratio of retained earnings to book value. This ratio would not in general provide an acceptable approximation to the "growth" variable of (12) in any sample in which firms resorted to external financing. Furthermore, even if by some chance a sample was found in which all firms relied entirely on retained earnings, his tests then could not settle the question of dividend policy. For if all firms financed investment internally (or used external financing only in strict proportion to internal financing as Gordon assumes in [8]) then there would be no way to distinguish between the effects of dividend policy and investment policy (see below p. 424).

frequently suggest.[11] It does, however, have the disadvantage in contrast with previous approaches of obscuring the role of dividend policy. In particular, uncritical use of the dividend approach has often led to the unwarranted inference that, since the investor is buying dividends and since dividend policy affects the amount of dividends, then dividend policy must also affect the current price.

Properly formulated, the dividend approach defines the current worth of a share as the discounted value of the stream of dividends to be paid on the share in perpetuity. That is

$$p(t) = \sum_{\tau=0}^{\infty} \frac{d(t + \tau)}{(1 + \rho)^{\tau+1}}. \tag{13}$$

To see the equivalence between this approach and previous ones, let us first restate (13) in terms of total market value as

$$V(t) = \sum_{\tau=0}^{\infty} \frac{D_t(t + \tau)}{(1 + \rho)^{\tau+1}}, \tag{14}$$

where $D_t(t + \tau)$ denotes that portion of the total dividends $D(t + \tau)$ paid during period $t + \tau$, that accrues to the shares of record as of the start of period t (indicated by the subscript). That equation (14) is equivalent to (9) and hence also to (12) is immediately apparent for the special case in which no outside financing is undertaken after period t, for in that case

$$D_t(t + \tau) = D(t + \tau) = X(t + \tau) - I(t + \tau).$$

To allow for outside financing, note that we can rewrite (14) as

$$V(t) = \frac{1}{1 + \rho} \left[D_t(t) + \sum_{\tau=1}^{\infty} \frac{D_t(t + \tau)}{(1 + \rho)^{\tau}} \right]$$

$$= \frac{1}{1 + \rho} \left[D(t) = \sum_{\tau=0}^{\infty} \frac{D_t(t + \tau + 1)}{(1 + \rho)^{\tau+1}} \right]. \tag{15}$$

---

[11]See, e.g., the classic statement of the position in J. B. Williams [21]. The equivalence of the dividend approach to many of the other standard approaches is noted to our knowledge only in our [16] and, by implication, in Bodenhorn [1].

The summation term in the last expression can be written as the difference between the stream of dividends accruing to all the shares of record as of $t + 1$ and that portion of the stream that will accrue to the shares newly issued in t, that is,

$$\sum_{\tau=0}^{\infty} \frac{D_t(t + \tau + 1)}{(1 + \rho)^{\tau+1}} = \left(1 - \frac{m(t + 1)}{n(t + 1)}\right) \sum_{\tau=0}^{\infty} \frac{D_{t+1}(t + \tau + 1)}{(1 + \rho)^{\tau+1}}. \tag{16}$$

But from (14) we know that the second summation in (16) is precisely $V(t + 1)$ so that (15) can be reduced to

$$V(t) = \frac{1}{1 + \rho} \left[D(t) + \left(1 - \frac{m(t + 1)p(t + 1)}{n(t + 1)p(t + 1)}\right) V(t + 1) \right]$$

$$= \frac{1}{1 + \rho} [D(t) + V(t + 1) - m(t + 1)p(t + 1)], \tag{17}$$

which is (3) and which has already been shown to imply both (9) and (12).[12]

There are, of course, other ways in which the equivalence of the dividend approach to the other approaches might have been established, but the method presented has the advantage perhaps of providing some further insight into the reason for the irrelevance of dividend policy. An increase in current dividends, given the firm's investment policy, must necessarily reduce the terminal value of existing shares because part of the future dividend stream that would otherwise have accrued to the existing shares must be diverted to attract the outside capital from which, in effect, the higher current dividends are paid. Under our basic assumptions, however, ρ must be the same for all investors, new as well as old. Consequently the market value of the dividends diverted to the outsiders, which is both the value of their contribution and the reduction in

---

[12] The statement that equations (9), (12), and (14) are equivalent must be qualified to allow for certain pathological extreme cases, fortunately of no real economic significance. An obvious example of such a case is the legendary company that is expected *never* to pay a dividend. If this were literally true then the value of the firm by (14) would be zero; by (9) it would be zero (or possibly negative since zero dividends rule out $X(t) > I(t)$ but not $X(t) < I(t)$); while by (12) the value might still be positive. What is involved here, of course, is nothing more than a discontinuity at zero since the value under (14) and (9) would be positive and the equivalence of both with (12) would hold if that value were also positive as long as there was some period T, however far in the future, beyond which the firm would pay out $\epsilon > 0$ per cent of its earnings, however small the value of ϵ.

terminal value of the existing shares, must always be precisely the same as the increase in current dividends.

The stream of earnings approach.—Contrary to widely held views, it is also possible to develop a meaningful and consistent approach to valuation running in terms of the stream of earnings generated by the corporation rather than of the dividend distributions actually made to the shareholders. Unfortunately, it is also extremely easy to mistake [*sic*] or misinterpret the earnings approach as would be the case if the value of the firm were to be defined as simply the discounted sum of future total earnings.[13] The trouble with such a definition is not, as is often suggested, that it overlooks the fact that the corporation is a separate entity and that these profits cannot freely be withdrawn by the shareholders; but rather that it neglects the fact that additional capital must be acquired at some cost to maintain the future earnings stream at its specified level. The capital to be raised in any future period is, of course, $I(t)$ and its opportunity cost, no matter how financed, is ρ per cent per period thereafter. Hence, the current value of the firm under the earnings approach must be stated as

$$V(0) = \sum_{t=0}^{\infty} \frac{1}{(1+\rho)^{t+1}} \left[X(t) - \sum_{\tau=0}^{t} \rho I(\tau) \right]. \tag{18}$$

That this version of the earnings approach is indeed consistent with our basic assumptions and equivalent to the previous approaches can be seen by regrouping terms and rewriting equation (18) as

$$V(0) = \sum_{t=0}^{\infty} \frac{1}{(1+\rho)^{t+1}} X(t) - \sum_{t=0}^{\infty} \left(\sum_{\tau=t}^{\infty} \frac{\rho I(t)}{(1+\rho)^{\tau+1}} \right)$$

$$= \sum_{t=0}^{\infty} \frac{1}{(1+\rho)^{t+1}} X(t) - \sum_{t=0}^{\infty} \frac{1}{(1+\rho)^{t+1}} \left(\sum_{\tau=0}^{\infty} \frac{\rho I(t)}{(1+\rho)^{\tau+1}} \right). \tag{19}$$

---

[13]In fairness, we should point out that there is no one, to our knowledge, who has seriously advanced this view. It is a view whose main function seems to be to serve as a "straw man" to be demolished by those supporting the dividend view. See, e.g., Gordon [9, esp. pp. 102-3]. Other writers take as the supposed earnings counter-view to the dividend approach not a relation running in terms of the *stream* of earnings but simply the proposition that price is proportional to current earnings, i.e., $V(0) = X(0)/\rho$. The probable origins of this widespread misconception about the earnings approach are discussed further below (p. 424).

Since the last inclosed summation reduces simply to $I(t)$, the expression (19) in turn reduces to simply

$$V(0) = \sum_{t=0}^{\infty} \frac{1}{(1 + \rho)^{t+1}} [X(t) - I(t)], \tag{20}$$

which is precisely our earlier equation (9).

Note that the version of the earnings approach presented here does not depend for its validity upon any special assumptions about the time shape of the stream of total profits or the stream of dividends per share. Clearly, however, the time paths of the two streams are closely related to each other (via financial policy) and to the stream of returns derived by holders of the shares. Since these relations are of some interest in their own right and since misunderstandings about them have contributed to the confusion over the role of dividend policy, it may be worthwhile to examine them briefly before moving on to relax the basic assumptions.

III.   Earnings, Dividends, and Growth Rates

The convenient case of constant growth rates.—The relation between the stream of earnings of the firm and the stream of dividends and of returns to the stockholders can be brought out most clearly by specializing (12) to the case in which investment opportunities are such as to generate a constant rate of growth of profits in perpetuity. Admittedly, this case has little empirical significance, but it is convenient for illustrative purposes and has received much attention in the literature.

Specifically, suppose that in each period t the firm has the opportunity to invest in real assets a sum $I(t)$ that is k per cent as large as its total earnings for the period; and that this investment produces a perpetual yield of ρ^* beginning with the next period. Then, by definition

$$X(t) = X(t - 1) + \rho^* I(t - 1) = X(t - 1)[1 + k\rho^*] = X(0)[1 + k\rho^*]^t \tag{21}$$

and $k\rho^*$ is the (constant) rate of growth of total earnings. Substituting from (21) into (12) for $I(t)$ we obtain

$$V(0) = \frac{X(0)}{\rho} + \sum_{t=0}^{\infty} \left(\frac{\rho^* - \rho}{\rho} \right) kX(0)[1 + k\rho^*]^t (1 + \rho)^{-(t+1)}$$

$$= \frac{X(0)}{\rho} \left[1 + \frac{k(\rho^* - \rho)}{1 + \rho} \sum_{t=0}^{\infty} \left(\frac{1 + k\rho^*}{1 + \rho} \right)^t \right]. \tag{22}$$

Evaluating the infinite sum and simplifying, we finally obtain [14]

$$V(0) = \frac{X(0)}{\rho} \left[1 + \frac{k(\rho^* - \rho)}{\rho - k\rho^*} \right] = \frac{X(0)(1 - k)}{\rho - k\rho^*}, \tag{23}$$

which expresses the value of the firm as a function of its current earnings, the rate of growth of earnings, the internal rate of return, and the market rate of return. [15] Note that (23) holds not just for period 0, but for every t. Hence if $X(t)$ is growing at the rate $k\rho^*$, it follows that the value of the enterprise, $V(t)$, also grows at that rate.

---

[14] One advantage of the specialization (23) is that it makes it easy to see what is really involved in the assumption here and throughout the paper that the $V(0)$ given by any of our summation formulas is necessarily finite (cf. above, n. 4). In terms of (23) the condition is clearly $k\rho^* < \rho$, i.e., that the rate of growth of the firm be less than market rate of discount. Although the case of (perpetual) growth rates greater than the discount factor is the much-discussed "growth stock praradox" [*sic*] (e.g. [6]), it has no real economic significance as we pointed out in [16, esp. n. 17, p. 664]. This will be apparent when one recalls that the discount rate ρ, though treated as a constant in partial equilibrium (relative price) analysis of the kind presented here, is actually a variable from the standpoint of the system as a whole. That is, if the assumption of finite value for all shares did not hold, because for some shares $k\rho^*$ was (perpetually) greater than ρ, then ρ would necessarily rise until an over-all equilibrium in the capital markets had been restored.

[15] An interesting and more realistic variant of (22), which also has a number of convenient features from the standpoint of developing empirical tests, can be obtained by assuming that the special investment opportunities are available not in perpetuity but only over some finite interval of T periods. To exhibit the value of the firm for this case, we need only replace the infinite summation in (22) with a summation running from $t = 0$ to $t = T - 1$. Evaluating the resulting expression, we obtain

$$V(0) = \frac{X(0)}{\rho} \left\{ 1 + \frac{k(\rho^* - \rho)}{\rho - k\rho^*} \left[1 - \left(\frac{1 + k\rho^*}{1 + \rho} \right)^T \right] \right\}. \tag{22a}$$

Note that (22a) holds even if $k\rho^* > \rho$, so that the so-called growth paradox disappears altogether. If, as we should generally expect, $(1 + k\rho^*)/(1 + \rho)$ is close to one, and if T is not too large, the right hand side of (22a) admits of a very convenient approximation. In this case in fact we can write

The growth of dividends and the growth of total profits.—Given that total earnings (and the total value of the firm) are growing at the rate $k\rho^*$ what is the rate of growth of dividends per share and of the price per share? Clearly, the answer will vary depending on whether or not the firm is paying out a high percentage of its earnings and thus relying heavily on outside financing. We can show the nature of this dependence explicitly by making use of the fact that whatever the rate of growth of dividends per share the present value of the firm by the dividend approach must be the same as by the earnings approach. Thus let

g = the rate of growth of dividends per share, or, what amounts to the same thing, the rate of growth of dividends accruing to the shares of the current holders (i.e., $D_0(t) = D_0(0)[1 + g]^t$);

k_r = the fraction of total profits retained in each period (so that $D(t) = X(0)[1 - k_r]$);

$k_e = k - k_r$ = the amount of external capital raised per period, expressed as a fraction of profits in the period.

Then the present value of the stream of dividends to the original owners will be

$$D_0(0) \sum_{t=0}^{\infty} \frac{(1+g)^t}{(1+\rho)^{t+1}} = \frac{D(0)}{\rho - g} = \frac{X(0)[1 - k_r]}{\rho - g}. \tag{24}$$

$$\left[\frac{1 + k\rho^*}{1 + \rho}\right]^T \cong 1 + T(k\rho^* - \rho)$$

the approximation holding, if, as we should expect, $(1 + k\rho^*)$ and $(1 + \rho)$ are both close to unity. Substituting this approximation into (22*a*) and simplifying, finally yields

$$V(0) \cong \frac{X(0)}{\rho}\left[1 + \frac{k(\rho^* - \rho)}{\rho - k\rho^*} T(\rho - k\rho^*)\right]$$

$$= \left[\frac{X(0)}{\rho} + kX(0)\left(\frac{\rho^* - \rho}{\rho}\right)T\right]. \tag{22b}$$

The common sense of (22*b*) is easy to see. The current value of a firm is given by the value of the earning power of the currently held assets plus the market value of the special earning opportunity multiplied by the number of years for which it is expected to last.

By virtue of the dividend approach we know that (24) must be equal to $V(0)$. If, therefore, we equate it to the right-hand side of (23), we obtain

$$\frac{X(0)[1 - k_r]}{\rho - g} = \frac{X(0)[1 - (k_r + k_e)]}{\rho - k\rho^*}$$

from which it follows that the rate of growth of dividends per share and the rate of growth of the price of a share must be[16]

$$g = k\rho^* \frac{1 - k_r}{1 - k} - k_e\rho \frac{1}{1 - k}. \tag{25}$$

Notice that in the extreme case in which all financing is internal ($k_e = 0$ and $k = k_r$), the second term drops out and the first becomes simply $k\rho^*$. Hence the growth rate of dividends in that special case is exactly the same as that of total profits and total value and is proportional to the rate of retention k_r. In all other cases, g is necessarily less than $k\rho^*$ and may even be negative, despite a positive $k\rho^*$, if $\rho^* < \rho$ and if the firm pays out a large fraction of its income in dividends. In the other direction, we see from (25) that even if a firm is a "growth" corporation ($\rho^* > \rho$) then the stream of dividends and price per share must grow over time even though $k_r = 0$, that is, even though it pays out *all* its earnings in dividends.

The relation between the growth rate of the firm and the growth rate of dividends under various dividend policies is illustrated graphically in Figure 1 in

---

[16]That g is the rate of price increase per share as well as the rate of growth of dividends per share follows from the fact that by (13) and the definition of g

$$p(t) = \sum_{\tau=0}^{\infty} \frac{d(t + \tau)}{(1 + \rho)^{\tau+1}}$$

$$= \sum_{\tau=0}^{\infty} \frac{d(0)[1 + g]^{t+\tau}}{(1 + \rho)^{\tau+1}}$$

$$= (1 + g)^t \sum_{\tau=0}^{\infty} \frac{d(\tau)}{(1 + \rho)^{\tau+1}}$$

$$= p(0)[1 + g]^t.$$

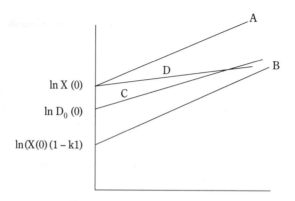

A. Total earnings: $\ln X(t) = \ln X(0) + k\rho^*t$;
B. Total earnings minus capital invested: $\ln [X(t) - I(t)] = \ln X(0)[1 - k] + k\rho^*t$;
   Dividends per share (all financing internal): $\ln D_0(t) = \ln D(0) + gt = \ln X(0)[1 - k] + k\rho^*t$;
C. Dividends per share (some financing external): $\ln D_0(t) = \ln D(0) + gt$;
D. Dividends per share (all financing external): $\ln D_0(t) = \ln X(0) + [(k/1 - k)(\rho^* - \rho)]t$.

Figure 1   Growth of dividends per share in relation to growth in total earnings

which for maximum clarity the natural logarithm of profits and dividends have been plotted against time. [17]

Line A shows the total earnings of the firm growing through time at the constant rate $k\rho^*$, the slope of A. Line B shows the growth of (1) the stream of total earnings minus capital outlays and (2) the stream of dividends to the original owners (or dividends per share) in the special case in which all financing is internal. The slope of B is, of course, the same as that of A and the (constant) difference between the curves is simply $\ln(1 - k)$, the ratio of dividends to profits. Line C shows the growth of dividends per share when the firm uses both internal and external financing. As compared with the pure retention case, the line starts higher but grows more slowly at the rate g given by (25). The higher the payout policy, the higher the starting position and the slower the growth up to the other limiting case of complete external financing, Line D, which starts at $\ln X(0)$ and grows at a rate of $(k/1 - k) \cdot (\rho^* - \rho)$.

---

[17]That is, we replace each discrete compounding expression such as $X(t) = X(0)[1 + k\rho^*]^t$ with its counterpart under continuous discounting $X(t) = X(0)e^{k\rho^*t}$ which, of course, yields the convenient linear relation $\ln X(t) = \ln X(0) + k\rho^*t$.

The special case of exclusively internal financing.—As noted above the growth rate of dividends per share is not the same as the growth rate of the firm except in the special case in which all financing is internal. This is merely one of a number of peculiarities of this special case on which, unfortunately, many writers have based their entire analysis. The reason for the preoccupation with this special case is far from clear to us. Certainly no one would suggest that it is the only empirically relevant case. Even if the case were in fact the most common, the theorist would still be under an obligation to consider alternative assumptions. We suspect that in the last analysis, the popularity of the internal financing model will be found to reflect little more than its ease of manipulation combined with the failure to push the analysis far enough to disclose how special and how treacherous a case it really is.

In particular, concentration on this special case appears to be largely responsible for the widely held view that, even under perfect capital markets, there is an optimum dividend policy for the firm that depends on the internal rate of return. Such a conclusion is almost inevitable if one works exclusively with the assumption, explicit or implicit, that funds for investment come *only* from retained earnings. For in that case *dividend policy* is indistinguishable from *investment policy*; and there *is* an optimal investment policy which does in general depend on the rate of return.

Notice also from (23) that if $\rho^* = \rho$ and $k = k_r$, the term $[1 - k_r]$ can be canceled from both the numerator and the denominator. The value of the firm becomes simply $X(0)/\rho$, the capitalized value of current earnings. Lacking a standard model for valuation more general than the retained earnings case it has been all too easy for many to conclude that this dropping out of the payout ratio $[1 - k_r]$ when $\rho^* = \rho$ must be what is meant by the irrelevance of dividend policy and that $V(0) = X(0)/\rho$ must constitute the "earnings" approach.

Still another example of the pitfalls in basing arguments on this special case is provided by the recent and extensive work on valuation by M. Gordon. [18] Gordon argues, in essense, that because of increasing uncertainty the discount rate $\hat{\rho}(t)$ applied by an investor to a future dividend payment will rise with t, where t denotes not a specific date but rather the distance from

---

[18]See esp. [8]. Gordon's views represent the most explicit and sophisticated formulation of what might be called the "bird-in-the-hand" fallacy. For other, less elaborate, statements of essentially the same position see, among others, Graham and Dodd [11, p. 433] and Clendenin and Van Cleave [3].

the period in which the investor performs the discounting. [19] Hence, when we use a single uniform discount rate ρ as in (22) or (23), this rate should be thought of as really an average of the "true" rates $\hat{\rho}(t)$ each weighted by the size of the expected dividend payment at time t. If the dividend stream is growing exponentially then such a weighted average ρ would, of course, be higher the greater the rate of growth of dividends g since the greater will then be the portion of the dividend stream arising in the distant as opposed to the near future. But if all financing is assumed to be internal, then $g = k_r \rho^*$ so that given ρ^*, the weighted average discount factor ρ will be an increasing function of the rate of retention k_r which would run counter to our conclusion that dividend policy has no effect on the current value of the firm or its cost of capital.

For all its ingenuity, however, and its seeming foundation in uncertainty, the argument clearly suffers fundamentally from the typical confounding of dividend policy with investment policy that so frequently accompanies use of the internal financing model. Had Gordon not confined his attention to this special case (or its equivalent variants), he would have seen that while a change in dividend policy will necessarily affect the size of the expected dividend payment on the share in any future period, it need not, in the general case, affect either the size of the *total* return that the investor expects during that period or the degree of uncertainty attaching to that total return. As should be abundantly clear by now, a change in dividend policy, given investment policy, implies a change only in the distribution of the total return in any period as between dividends and capital gains. If investors behave rationally, such a change cannot affect market valuations. Indeed, if they valued shares according to the Gordon approach and thus paid a premium for higher payout ratios, then holders of the low payout shares would actually realize consistently higher returns on their investment over any stated interval of time. [20]

---

[19]We use the notation $\hat{\rho}(t)$ to avoid any confusion between Gordon's purely subjective discount rate and the objective, market-given yields $\rho(t)$ in Sec. I above. To attempt to derive valuation formulas under uncertainty from these purely subjective discount factors involves, of course, an error essentially analogous to that of attempting to develop the certainty formulas from "marginal rates of time preference" rather than objective market opportunities.

[20]This is not to deny that growth stocks (in our sense) may well be "riskier" than non-growth stocks. But to the extent that this is true, it will be due to the possibly greater uncertainty attaching to the size and duration of future growth opportunities and hence to the size of the future stream of total returns quite apart from any questions of dividend policy.

Corporate earnings and investor returns.—Knowing the relation of g to $k\rho^*$ we can answer a question of considerable interest to economic theorists, namely: What is the precise relation between the earnings of the corporation in any period $X(t)$ and the total return to the owners of the stock during that period?[21] If we let $G_t(t)$ be the capital gains to the owners during t, we know that

$$D_t(t) + G_t(t) = X(t)(1 - k_r) + gV(t) \tag{26}$$

since the rate of growth of price is the same as that of dividends per share. Using (25) and (26) to substitute for g and $V(t)$ and simplifying, we find that

$$D_t(t) + G_t(t) = X(t)\left[\frac{\rho(1 - k)}{\rho - k\rho^*}\right]. \tag{27}$$

The relation between the investors' return and the corporation's profits is thus seen to depend entirely on the relation between ρ^* and ρ. If $\rho^* = \rho$ (i.e., the firm has no special "growth" opportunities), then the expression in brackets becomes 1 and the investor returns are precisely the same as the corporate profits. If $\rho^* < \rho$, however, the investors' return will be less than the corporate

---

[21]Note also that the above analysis enables us to deal very easily with the familiar issue of whether a firm's cost of equity capital is measured by its earnings/price ratio or by its dividend/price ratio. Clearly, the answer is that it is measured by neither, except under very special circumstances. For from (23) we have for the earnings/price ratio

$$\frac{X(0)}{V(0)} = \frac{\rho - k\rho^*}{1 - k},$$

which is equal to the cost of capital ρ, only if the firm has no growth potential (i.e., $\rho^* = \rho$). And from (24) we have for the dividend/price ratio

$$\frac{D(0)}{V(0)} = \rho - g,$$

which is equal to ρ only when $g = 0$; i.e., from (25), either when $k = 0$; or, if $k > 0$, when $\rho^* < \rho$ and the amount of external financing is precisely

$$k_e = \frac{\rho^*}{\rho} k[1 - k_r],$$

so that the gain from the retention of earnings exactly offsets the loss that would otherwise be occasioned by the unprofitable investment.

earnings; and, in the case of growth corporations the investors' return will actually be greater than the flow of corporate profits over the interval. [22]

Some implications for constructing empirical tests.—Finally the fact that we have two different (though not independent) measures of growth in $k\rho^*$ and g and two corresponding families of valuation formulas means, among other things, that we can proceed by either of two routes in empirical studies of valuation. We can follow the standard practice of the security analyst and think in terms of price per share, dividends per share, and the rate of growth of dividends per share; or we can think in terms of the total value of the enterprise, total earnings, and the rate of growth of total earnings. Our own preference happens to be for the second approach primarily because certain additional variables of interest—such as dividend policy, leverage, and size of firm—can be incorporated more easily and meaningfully into test equations in which the growth term is the growth of total earnings. But this can wait. For present purposes, the thing to be stressed is simply that two approaches, properly carried through, are in no sense *opposing* views of the valuation process; but rather equivalent views, with the choice between them largely a matter of taste and convenience.

---

[22]The above relation between earnings per share and dividends plus capital gains also means that there will be a systematic relation between retained earnings and capital gains. The "marginal" relation is easy to see and is always precisely one for one regardless of growth or financial policy. That is, taking a dollar away from dividends and adding it to retained earnings (all other things equal) means an increase in capital gains of one dollar (or a reduction in capital loss of one dollar). The "average" relation is somewhat more complex. From (26) and (27) we can see that

$$G_t(t) = k_r X(t) + kX(t) \frac{\rho^* - \rho}{\rho - k\rho^*}.$$

Hence, if $\rho^* = \rho$ the total capital gain received will be exactly the same as the total retained earnings per share. For growth corporations, however, the capital gain will always be greater than the retained earnings (and there will be a capital gain of

$$kX(t) \left[\frac{\rho^* - \rho}{\rho - k\rho^*} \right]$$

even when all earnings are paid out). For non-growth corporations the relation between gain and retentions is reversed. Note also that the absolute difference between the total capital gain and the total retained earnings is a constant (given, ρ, k and ρ^*) unaffected by dividend policy. Hence the *ratio* of capital gain to retained earnings will vary directly with the payout ratio for growth corporations (and vice versa for non-growth corporations). This means, among other things, that it is dangerous to attempt to draw inferences about the relative growth potential or relative managerial efficiency of corporations solely on the basis of the ratio of capital gains to retained earnings (cf. Harkavy [12, esp. pp. 289–94]).

IV.   The Effects of Dividend Policy under Uncertainty

Uncertainty and the general theory of valuation.—In turning now from the ideal world of certainty to one of uncertainty our first step, alas, must be to jettison the fundamental valuation principle as given, say, in our equation (3)

$$V(t) = \frac{1}{1 + \rho(t)} \left[D(t) + n(t)p(t + 1) \right]$$

and from which the irrelevance proposition as well as all the subsequent valuation formulas in Sections II and III were derived. For the terms in the bracket can no longer be regarded as given numbers, but must be recognized as "random variables" from the point of view of the investor as of the start of period t. Nor is it at all clear what meaning can be attached to the discount factor $1/[1 + \rho(t)]$ since what is being discounted is not a given return, but at best only a probability distribution of possible returns. We can, of course, delude ourselves into thinking that we are preserving equation (3) by the simple and popular expedient of drawing a bar over each term and referring to it thereafter as the mathematical expectation of the random variable. But except for the trivial case of universal linear utility functions we know that $V(t)$ would also be affected, and materially so, by the higher order moments of the distribution of returns. Hence there is no reason to believe that the discount factor for expected values, $1/[1 + \rho(t)]$, would in fact be the same for any two firms chosen arbitrarily, not to mention that the expected values themselves may well be different for different investors.

All this is not to say, of course, that there are insuperable difficulties in the way of developing a testable theory of rational market valuation under uncertainty.[23] On the contrary, our investigations of the problem to date have convinced us that it is indeed possible to construct such a theory—though the construction, as can well be imagined, is a fairly complex and space-consuming task. Fortunately, however, this task need not be undertaken in this paper which is concerned primarily with the effects of dividend policy on market

---

[23]Nor does it mean that all the previous certainty analysis has no relevance whatever in the presence of uncertainty. There are many issues, such as those discussed in Sec. I and II, that really relate only to what has been called the pure "futurity" component in valuation. Here, the valuation formulas can still be extremely useful in maintaining the internal consistency of the reasoning and in suggesting (or criticizing) empirical tests of certain classes of hypotheses about valuation, even though the formulas themselves cannot be used to grind out precise numerical values for specific real-world shares.

valuation. For even without a full-fledged theory of what *does* determine market value under uncertainty we can show that dividend policy at least is *not* one of the determinants. To establish this particular generalization of the previous certainty results we need only invoke a corresponding generalization of the original postulate of rational behavior to allow for the fact that, under uncertainty, choices depend on expectations as well as tastes.

"Imputed rationality" and "symmetric market rationality."—This generalization can be formulated in two steps as follows. First, we shall say that an individual trader "imputes rationality to the market" or satisfies the postulate of "imputed rationality" if, in forming expectations, he assumes that every other trader in the market is (*a*) rational in the previous sense of preferring more wealth to less regardless of the form an increment in wealth may take, and (*b*) imputes rationality to all other traders. Second, we shall say that a market as a whole satisfies the postulate of "symmetric market rationality" if every trader both behaves rationally and imputes rationality to the market. [24]

Notice that this postulate of symmetric market rationality differs from the usual postulate of rational behavior in several important respects. In the first place, the new postulate covers not only the choice behavior of individuals but also their expectations of the choice behavior of others. Second, the postulate is a statement about the market as a whole and not just about individual behavior. Finally, though by no means least, symmetric market rationality cannot be deduced from individual rational behavior in the usual sense since that sense does not imply imputing rationality to others. It may, in fact, imply a choice behavior consistent with imputed rationality unless the individual actually believes the market to be symmetrically rational. For if an ordinarily rational investor had good reason to believe that other investors would not behave rationally, then it might well be rational for him to adopt a strategy he would otherwise have rejected as irrational. Our postulate thus rules out, among other things, the possibility of speculative "bubbles" wherein an individually rational investor buys a security he knows to be overpriced (i.e., too expensive in

---

[24] We offer the term "symmetric market rationality" with considerable diffidence and only after having been assured by game theorists that there is no accepted term for this concept in the literature of that subject even though the postulate itself (or close parallels to it) does appear frequently. In the literature of economics a closely related, but not exact counterpart is Muth's "hypothesis of rational expectations" [18]. Among the more euphonic, though we feel somewhat less revealing, alternatives that have been suggested to us are "putative rationality" (by T. J. Koopmans), "bi-rationality" (by G. L. Thompson), "empathetic rationality" (by Andrea Modigliani), and "pan-rationality" (by A. Ando).

relation to its expected *long-run* return to be attractive as a permanent addition to his portfolio) in the expectation that he can resell it at a still more inflated price before the bubble bursts. [25]

The irrelevance of dividend policy despite uncertainty.—In Section I we were able to show that, given a firm's investment policy, its dividend policy was irrelevant to its current market valuation. We shall now show that this fundamental conclusion need not be modified merely because of the presence of uncertainty about the future course of profits, investment, or dividends (assuming again, as we have throughout, that investment policy can be regarded as separable from dividend policy). To see that uncertainty about these elements changes nothing essential, consider a case in which current investors believe that the future streams of total earnings and total investment whatever actual values they may assume at different points in time will be identical for two firms, 1 and 2. [26] Suppose further, provisionally, that the same is believed to be true of future total dividend payments from period one on so that the only way in which the two firms differ is possibly with respect to the prospective dividend in the current period, period 0. In terms of previous notation we are thus assuming that

$$\bar{X}_1(t) = \bar{X}_2(t) \qquad t = 0 \ldots \infty$$

$$\bar{I}_1(t) = \bar{I}_2(t) \qquad t = 0 \ldots \infty$$

$$\bar{D}_1(t) = \bar{D}_2(t) \qquad t = 1 \ldots \infty$$

---

[25] We recognize, of course, that such speculative bubbles have actually arisen in the past (and will probably continue to do so in the future), so that our postulate can certainly not be taken to be of universal applicability. We feel, however, that it is also not of universal inapplicability since from our observation, speculative bubbles, though well publicized when they occur, do not seem to us to be a dominant, or even a fundamental, feature of actual market behavior under uncertainty. That is, we would be prepared to argue that, as a rule and on the average, markets do not behave in ways which do not obviously contradict the postulate so that the postulate may still be useful, at least as a first approximation, for the analysis of long-run tendencies in organized capital markets. Needless to say, whether our confidence in the postulate is justified is something that will have to be determined by empirical tests of its implications (such as, of course, the irrelevance of dividend policy).

[26] The assumption of two identical firms is introduced for convenience of exposition only, since it usually is easier to see the implications of rationality when there is an explicit arbitrage mechanism, in this case, switches between the shares of the two firms. The assumption, however, is not necessary and we can, if we like, think of the two firms as really corresponding to two states of the same firm for an investor performing a series of "mental experiments" on the subject of dividend policy.

the subscripts indicating the firms and the tildes being added to the variables to indicate that these are to be regarded from the standpoint of current period, not as known numbers but as numbers that will be drawn in the future from the appropriate probability distributions. We may now ask: "What will be the return, $\tilde{R}_1(0)$ to the current shareholders in firm 1 during the current period?" Clearly, it will be

$$\tilde{R}_1(0) = \tilde{D}_1(0) + \tilde{V}_1(1) - \tilde{m}_1(1)\tilde{p}_1(1). \tag{28}$$

But the relation between $\tilde{D}_1(0)$ and $\tilde{m}_1(1)\tilde{p}_1(1)$ is necessarily still given by equation (4) which is merely an accounting identity so that we can write

$$\tilde{m}_1(1)\tilde{p}_1(1) = \tilde{I}_1(0) - [\tilde{X}_1(0) - \tilde{D}_1(0)], \tag{29}$$

and, on substituting in (28), we obtain

$$\tilde{R}_1(0) = \tilde{X}_1(0) - \tilde{I}_1(0) + \tilde{V}_1(1) \tag{30}$$

for firm 1. By an exactly parallel process we can obtain an equivalent expression for $\tilde{R}_2(0)$.

Let us now compare $\tilde{R}_1(0)$ with $\tilde{R}_2(0)$. Note first that, by assumption, $\tilde{X}_1(0) = \tilde{X}_2(0)$ and $\tilde{I}_1(0) = \tilde{I}_2(0)$. Furthermore, with symmetric market rationality, the terminal values $\tilde{V}_i(1)$ can depend only on prospective future earnings, investment and dividends from period 1 on and these too, by assumption, are identical for the two companies. Thus symmetric rationality implies that every investor must expect $\tilde{V}_1(1) = \tilde{V}_2(1)$ and hence finally $\tilde{R}_1(0) = \tilde{R}_2(0)$. But if the return to the investors is the same in the two cases, rationality requires that the two firms command the same current value so that $\tilde{V}_1(0)$ must equal $\tilde{V}_2(0)$ regardless of any difference in dividend payments during period 0. Suppose now that we allow dividends to differ not just in period 0 but in period 1 as well, but still retain the assumption of equal $\tilde{X}_i(t)$ and $\tilde{I}_i(t)$ in all periods and of equal $\tilde{D}_i(t)$ in period 2 and beyond. Clearly, the only way differences in dividends in period 1 can effect [sic] $\tilde{R}_i(0)$ and hence $\tilde{V}_i(0)$ is via $\tilde{V}_i(1)$. But, by the assumption of symmetric market rationality, current investors know that as of the start of period 1 the then investors will value the two firms rationally and we have already shown that differences in the current dividend do not affect current value. Thus we must have $\tilde{V}_1(1) = \tilde{V}_2(1)$—and hence $\tilde{V}_1(0) = \tilde{V}_2(0)$—regardless of any possible difference in dividend payments during period 1. By an obvious extension of the reasoning to $\tilde{V}_i(2)$, $\tilde{V}_i(3)$, and so on, it must follow that the current valuation is unaffected by differences in dividend payments in *any* future period and thus that dividend policy is irrelevant for the determination of market prices, given investment policy.[27]

Dividend policy and leverage.—A study of the above line of proof will show it to be essentially analogous to the proof for the certainty world, in which as we know, firms can have, in effect, only two alternative sources of investment funds: retained earnings or stock issues. In an uncertain world, however, there is the additional financing possibility of debt issues. The question naturally arises, therefore, as to whether the conclusion about irrelevance remains valid even in the presence of debt financing, particularly since there may very well be interactions between debt policy and dividend policy. The answer is that it does, and while a complete demonstration would perhaps be too tedious and repetitious at this point, we can at least readily sketch out the main outlines of how the proof proceeds. We begin, as above, by establishing the conditions from period 1 on that lead to a situation in which $\bar{V}_1(1)$ must be brought into equality with $\bar{V}_2(1)$ where the V, following the approach in our earlier paper [17], is now to be interpreted as the total market value of the firm, debt plus equity, not merely equity alone. The return to the original investors taken as a whole—and remember that any individual always has the option of buying a proportional share of both the equity and the debt—must correspondingly be broadened to allow for the interest on the debt. There will also be a corresponding broadening of the accounting identity (4) to allow, on the one hand, for the interest return and, on the other, for any debt funds used to finance the investment in whole or in part. The net result is that both the dividend component and the interest component of total earnings will cancel out making the relevant (total) return, as before, $[\bar{X}_i(0) - \bar{I}_i(0) + \bar{V}_i(1)]$ which is clearly independent of the current dividend. It follows, then, that the value of the firm must also therefore be independent of dividend policy given investment policy.[28]

---

[27] We might note that the assumption of symmetric market rationality is sufficient to derive this conclusion but not strictly necessary if we are willing to weaken the irrelevance proposition to one running in terms of long-run, average tendencies in the market. Individual rationality alone could conceivably bring about the latter, for over the long pull rational investors could enforce this result by buying and holding "undervalued" securities because this would insure them higher long-run returns when eventually the prices became the same. They might, however, have a long, long wait.

[28] This same conclusion must also hold for the current market value of all the shares (and hence for the current price per share), which is equal to the total market value minus the given initially outstanding debt. Needless to say, however, the price per share and the value of the equity at *future* points in time will not be independent of dividend and debt policies in the interim.

The informational content of dividends.—To conclude our discussion of dividend policy under uncertainty, we might take note briefly of a common confusion about the meaning of the irrelevance proposition occasioned by the fact that in the real world a change in the dividend rate is often followed by a change in the market price (sometimes spectacularly so). Such a phenomenon would not be incompatible with irelevance [*sic*] to the extent that it was merely a reflection of what might be called the "informational content" of dividends, an attribute of particular dividend payments hitherto excluded by assumption from the discussion and proofs. That is, where a firm has adopted a policy of dividend stabilization with a long-established and generally appreciated "target payout ratio," investors are likely to (and have good reason to) interpret a change in the dividend rate as a change in management's views of future profit prospects for the firm.[29] The dividend change, in other words, provides the occasion for the price change though not its cause, the price still being solely a reflection of future earnings and growth opportunities. In any particular instance, of course, the investors might well be mistaken in placing this interpretation on the dividend change, since the management might really only be changing its payout target or possibly even attempting to "manipulate" the price. But this would involve no particular conflict with the irrelevance proposition, unless, of course, the price changes in such cases were not reversed when the unfolding of events had made clear the true nature of the situation.[30]

V. Dividend Policy and Market Imperfections

To complete the analysis of dividend policy, the logical next step would presumably be to abandon the assumption of perfect capital markets. This is, however, a good deal easier to say than to do principally because there is no unique set of circumstances that constitutes "imperfection." We can describe not one but a multitude of possible departures from strict perfection, singly and in combinations. Clearly, to attempt to pursue the implications of each of these would only serve to add inordinately to an already overlong discussion. We shall instead, therefore, limit ourselves in this concluding section to a few brief and

---

[29]For evidence on the prevalence of dividend stabilization and target ratios see Lintner [15].

[30]For a further discussion of the subject of the informational content of dividends, including its implications for empirical tests of the irrelevance proposition, see Modigliani and Miller [16, pp. 666–68].

general observations about imperfect markets that we hope may prove helpful to those taking up the task of extending the theory of valuation in this direction.

First, it is important to keep in mind that from the standpoint of dividend policy, what counts is not imperfection per se but only imperfection that might lead an investor to have a systematic preference as between a dollar of current dividends and a dollar of current capital gains. Where no such systematic preference is produced, we can subsume the imperfection in the (random) error term always carried along when applying propositions derived from ideal models to real-world events.

Second, even where we do find imperfections that bias individual preferences—such as the existence of brokerage fees which tend to make young "accumulators" prefer low-payout shares and retired persons lean toward "income stocks"—such imperfections are at best only necessary but not sufficient conditions for certain payout policies to command a permanent premium in the market. If, for example, the frequency distribution of corporate payout ratios happened to correspond exactly with the distribution of investor preferences for payout ratios, then the existence of these preferences would clearly lead ultimately to a situation whose implications were different in no fundamental respect from the perfect market case. Each corporation would tend to attract to itself a "clientele" consisting of those preferring its particular payout ratio, but one clientele would be entirely as good as another in terms of the valuation it would imply for the firm. Nor, of course, is it necessary for the distributions to match exactly for this result to occur. Even if there were a "shortage" of some particular payout ratio, investors would still normally have the option of achieving their particular saving objectives without paying a premium for the stocks in short supply simply by buying appropriately weighted combinations of the more plentiful payout ratios. In fact, given the great range of corporate payout ratios known to be available, this process would fail to eliminate permanent premiums and discounts only if the distribution of investor preferences were heavily concentrated at either of the extreme ends of the payout scale.[31]

Of all the many market imperfections that might be detailed, the only one

---

[31] The above discussion should explain why, among other reasons, it would not be possible to draw any valid inference about the relative preponderance of "accumulators" as opposed to "income" buyers or the strength of their preferences merely from the weight attaching to dividends in a simple cross-sectional regression between value and payouts (as is attempted in Clendenin [2, p. 50] or Durand [5, p. 651]).

that would seem to be even remotely capable of producing such a concentration is the substantial advantage accorded to capital gains as compared with dividends under the personal income tax. Strong as this tax push toward capital gains may be for high-income individuals, however, it should be remembered that a substantial (and growing) fraction of total shares outstanding is currently held by investors for whom there is either no tax differential (charitable and educational institutions, foundations, pension trusts, and low-income retired individuals) or where the tax advantage is, if anything, in favor of dividends (casualty insurance companies and taxable corporations generally). Hence, again, the "clientele effect" will be at work. Furthermore, except for taxable individuals in the very top brackets, the required difference in before-tax yields to produce equal after-tax yields is not particularly striking, at least for moderate variations in the composition of returns. [32] All this is not to say, of course, that differences in yields (market values) caused by differences in payout policies should be ignored by managements or investors merely because they may be relatively small. But it may help to keep investigators from being too surprised if it turns out to be hard to measure or even to detect any premium for low-payout shares on the basis of standard statistical techniques.

Finally, we may note that since the tax differential in favor of capital gains is undoubtedly the major *systematic* imperfection in the market, one clearly cannot invoke "imperfections" to account for the difference between our irrelevance proposition and the standard view as to the role of dividend policy found in the literature of finance. For the standard view is not that low-payout companies command a premium; but that, in general, they will sell at a discount! [33] If such indeed were the case—and we, at least, are not prepared to concede that this has been established—then the analysis presented in this

---

[32] For example, if a taxpayer is subject to a marginal rate of 40 per cent on dividends and half that or 20 per cent on long-term capital gains, then a before-tax yield of 6 per cent consisting of 40 per cent dividends and 60 per cent capital gains produces an after-tax yield of 4.32 per cent. To net the same after-tax yield on a stock with 60 per cent of the return in dividends and only 40 per cent in capital gains would require a before-tax yield of 6.37 per cent. The difference would be somewhat smaller if we allowed for the present dividend credit, though it should also be kept in mind that the tax on capital gains may be avoided entirely under present arrangements if the gains are not realized during the holder's lifetime.

[33] See, among many, many others, Gordon [8, 9], Graham and Dodd [11, esp. chaps. xxxiv and xxxvi], Durand [4, 5], Hunt, Williams, and Donaldson [13, pp. 647-49], Fisher [7], Gordon and Shapiro [10], Harkavy [12], Clendenin [2], Johnson, Shapiro, and O'Meara [14], and Walter [19].

paper suggests there would be only one way to account for it; namely, as the result of systematic irrationality on the part of the investing public. [34]

To say that an observed positive premium on high payouts was due to irrationality would not, of course, make the phenomenon any less real. But it would at least suggest the need for a certain measure of caution by long-range policymakers. For investors, however naive they may be when they enter the market, do sometimes learn from experience; and perhaps, occasionally, even from reading articles such as this.

References

1. Bodenhorn, Diran. "On the Problem of Capital Budgeting," *Journal of Finance*, XIV (December, 1959), 473–92.

2. Clendenin, John. "What Do Stockholders Like?" *California Management Review*, I (Fall, 1958), 47–55.

3. Clendenin, John, and Van Cleave, M. "Growth and Common Stock Values," *Journal of Finance*, IX (September, 1954), 365–76.

4. Durand, David. *Bank Stock Prices and the Bank Capital Problem.* ("Occasional Paper," No. 54.) New York: National Bureau of Economic Research, 1957.

5. ————. "The Cost of Capital and the Theory of Investment: Comment," *American Economic Review*, XLIX (September, 1959), 639–54.

6. ————. "Growth Stocks and the Petersburg Paradox," *Journal of Finance*, XII (September, 1957), 348–63.

7. Fisher, G. R. "Some Factors Influencing Share Prices," *Economic Journal*, LXXI, No. 281 (March, 1961), 121–41.

8. Gordon, Myron. "Corporate Saving, Investment and Share Prices," *Review of Economics and Statistics* (forthcoming).

9. ————. "Dividends, Earnings and Stock Prices," *ibid.*, XLI, No. 2, Part I (May, 1959), 99–105.

---

[34] Or, less plausibly, that there is a systematic tendency for external funds to be used more productively than internal funds.

10. Gordon, Myron, and Shapiro, Eli. "Capital Equipment Analysis: The Required Rate of Profit," *Management Science*, III, 1956, 102–10.

11. Graham, Benjamin, and Dodd, David. *Security Analysis*. 3d ed. New York: McGraw–Hill Book Co., 1951.

12. Harkavy, Oscar. "The Relation between Retained Earnings and Common Stock Prices for Large Listed Corporations," *Journal of Finance*, VIII (September, 1953), 283–97.

13. Hunt, Pearson, Williams, Charles, and Donaldson, Gordon. *Basic Business Finance*. Homewood, Ill.: Richard D. Irwin, 1958.

14. Johnson, L. R., Shapiro, Eli, and O'Meara, J. "Valuation of Closely Held Stock for Federal Tax Purposes: Approach to an Objective Method," *University of Pennsylvania Law Review*, C, 166–95.

15. Lintner, John. "Distribution of Incomes of Corporations among Dividends, Retained Earnings and Taxes," *American Economic Review*, XLVI (May, 1956), 97–113.

16. Modigliani, Franco, and Miller, Merton. " 'The Cost of Capital, Corporation Finance and the Theory of Investment,': Reply," *American Economic Review*, XLIX (September, 1959), 655–69.

17. ———. "The Cost of Capital, Corporation Finance and the Theory of Investment," *ibid.*, XLVIII (1958), 261–97.

18. Muth, John F. "Rational Expectations and the Theory of Price Movements," *Econometrica* (forthcoming).

19. Walter, James E. "A Discriminant Function for Earnings-Price Ratios of Large Industrial Corporations," *Review of Economics and Statistics*, XLI (February, 1959), 44–52.

20. ———. "Dividend Policies and Common Stock Prices," *Journal of Finance*, XI (March, 1956), 29–41.

21. Williams, John B. *The Theory of Investment Value*. Cambridge, Mass.: Harvard University Press, 1938.